THE AMBITIOUS WOMAN IN BUSINESS

THE AMBITIOUS WOMAN IN BUSINESS

by

ELEANOR GILBERT

GYAN

Published by

Gyan Publishing House
5, Ansari Road
Daryaganj, New Delhi-110002
Phone: 011-47034999, 9811692060
E-mail: books@gyanbooks.com

Distribution Network
gyanbooks.com
India, USA, Canada, UK, Australia, France

ISBN : 978-81-212-6178-4 (PB)
First Published, 1916

2nd Impression 2021

Printed at: Gyan Press, Delhi.

The Ambitious Woman in Business
Author: Eleanor Gilbert

SCHOOLROOM IN A LARGE CORPORATION

THE AMBITIOUS WOMAN IN BUSINESS

By

ELEANOR GILBERT

CONTENTS

PART I—BUSINESS PRACTISE AND PERSONAL WELFARE

PART II—OCCUPATIONAL

CONTENTS

PREFACE

"How can I succeed in business?" In varied form the question comes to me daily, sometimes from eager young women about to enter a vocation; sometimes from experienced business women ambitious to get out of a rut; and sometimes from middle-aged women in desperate confession of failure.

What kind of success? Do you mean a large salary? Or do you want a responsible position, full of congenial work, honor and opportunity? Do you mean a pleasant, well-paying job that you can hold for a few years until you marry? Do you hope to embark in a business of your own? Have you the exceptionally intense ambition for wealth and power that developed a Hill, a Harriman, a Rockefeller?

Whenever I offer these inquiries, it becomes apparent immediately that the average woman has no definite goal for her business life, and that the relation of her business to her future is most vague. She is even frightened when it is suggested that she can begin to equip herself for great commercial power; but she is always interested in infantile "advice to business girls," on the less important issues of dress and deportment. Theoretically she clamors for "equal opportunity and equal pay for equal work," but actually her mental attitude toward work is wholly different from men. She is quite content if she is a decently paid member of the great class of permanent subordinates in business.

My purpose has been to present facts which will determine whether it is reasonable or desirable for a woman to entertain the same high goal in business as a man; and also, to bring intimately to her attention the modern methods used by men to achieve great success in business, which she can apply in planning her own future.

This book does not pretend to act as guide in the secret passages leading to that coveted goal—an easy job with heavy pay; nor does it offer an infallible patent medicine guaranteed to secure power or wealth. It is written out of a varied, every-day business experience; from reports of the trials and triumphs of other business women; and from interviews with employers.

I am writing it for the girl who plans to enter business life; for the college woman seeking a means of livelihood in some non-professional, non-teaching occupation. Business needs the college-bred woman, and I believe that the young woman of the future will take her college course for general culture preparatory to entering business just as our best type young men do to-day. The book is also for the woman in the home who feels the need or desire for economic independence, but does not know business requirements and perhaps feels somewhat conscience-stricken that she should desire to "desert" her home duties, even in part.

Chiefly I am writing it becanse I am convinced, from my investigations, that you, the typical American business woman, can be happy and successful both in business and as a many-sided, interesting woman. Unless you have unusual advantages, you are not shouldering as much responsibility as you are capable of carrying; you are not receiving as much in honor and pay as you could make yourself worth; you are not demanding enough of yourself; you are not developing latent abilities; you are not enjoying all the happiness that could be yours. And happiness, on a firm foundation, has a large place in the life of the most hard-working, most "tired business woman."

If you disagree, if you are of the favored few outside my group, lay down this book. It can not tell you more than you already know. But if you are ambitious for greater self-development or happiness, you may find some suggestion in the following pages.

ANN ROSENBLATT,
(*Eleanor Gilbert.*)

New York, *June* 8, 1916.

PART I

Business Practise and Personal Welfare

I

WHY WOMEN ARE IN BUSINESS

"WOMEN go to business because they consider it the modern marriage market," declared an English writer. Business men haven't time to flock to all the social functions that women devise to attract marriageable couples; so the ladies pursue the elusive eligible into the business world. "Women work for pin-money and fine clothes," is an idea exprest so frequently that it is almost a bromidiom. "Women are in business because they prefer any work to housework," is another typical opinion of the cynical male.

In fact, whenever there is public or private discussion of women in business, there are sure to arise reactionaries, of both sexes, who urge that woman's place is not in business, and who attribute her presence there only to selfish or inconsequential motives. On the other hand, there are extremists who affirm that first, last and all the time, the place of the intelligent woman is in a paid occupation outside the home. The entire subject is involved in so many highly radical and highly conservative opinions that it is difficult to determine which is the voice of wisdom. It may, therefore, be illuminating to consider: (1) Why are women in business; and (2) Ought women to be in business? In other words, is it necessary for women to be in business, and is business a good thing for women, for business, and for the family?

In order to get impartial opinion on the first subject, I invited discussion in the columns of newspapers like the New York *Evening Sun*, Philadelphia *Public Ledger*, simultaneously obtaining personal expressions direct from women who work as well as from employers of women. The conclusions based on these statements can be accepted only as estimates of the situation because a complete and accurate census seems impossible. Nevertheless, as letters and personal views come from women in many occupations — office, store, factory, studio—as well as from employers in such places, the summarized opinions are probably as shrewd and trustworthy a view of the situation as is obtainable at present.

Of course, there were extremes of opinion. There was the man who estimated that 95 per cent. of the women who worked were in business through sheer necessity. They had to work to keep from starving. Equally emphatic was the gentleman who declared that all women had no other purpose in work than clothes, as obviously most of their salaries went to buy ostrich plumes, chiffons and cosmetics.

But, after sifting letters and verbal opinions, the weight of evidence indicated that probably 85 per cent. of all the women who work in office, factory, shop, store and studio, work because it is necessary for them to do so to support themselves or their dependent families. These 85 per cent. are divided into the first four of the following groups; the remaining 15 per cent. are at work because of one or more of the last six reasons:

TEN REASONS WHY WOMEN GO TO BUSINESS

(1) They have no private incomes, and their men folk are unable or unwilling to support them,

(2) They must contribute to the support of a large or dependent family.

(3) They desire to help a husband who can not support the family in decent comfort on his own earnings.

(4) They desire a higher standard of living than the standard with which their parents are satisfied.

85%

(5) While the parents have a comfortable home, they are unable to supply adult daughters with pin-money, good clothes, entertaining, etc.

(6) There is not sufficient work in the home to keep the girl interested.

(7) Love of an occupation for which a woman thinks she is fitted.

(8) Desire to be economically independent even when she can be supported at home.

(9) Desire for business training so as to be self-supporting in case of need.

(10) The supposed opportunity for meeting in business marriageable men.

15%

WHY WOMEN ARE IN BUSINESS

When you compare the facts obtainable on the average income of American families, it is easy to see why the majority of adult women who work must support themselves, or contribute to the support of a family. The Government Census gives no statistics on total incomes, but estimates made[1] show that almost half the families in this country have an income of less than $15 per week on which to support an average family of four or five people, that is, father, mother and two or three children. Then, too, there are hundreds of thousands of women who have no one to rely upon for support, and hundreds of thousands of women, married and unmarried, who have one or more dependents. These facts indicate some of the reasons why women are in business.

Consider then, the second question: Ought woman to be in business, taking into account her destiny as a mother, and modern ideals

[1] Mahin's Data Book estimates the probable income of the total population as:

46.3% earn less than $15 a week
27.3% earn between $15 and $20 a week
10.4% earn between $24 and $30 a week
9.2% earn between $30 and $60 a week
6.8% earn over $60 per week

of life? What of the girl who has a home, and who is part of the family with the small income? "Why should she work?" is often asked, because "even $15 a week is sufficient to support a whole family, if the girl is content to live in the style to which her parents are accustomed."

Aye, there's the rub! She is *not* content. Standards of living grow higher each year in quite the same proportion as the cost of living. Mary wants to rise above the surroundings in which she was reared. She is ambitious for more of the comforts and refinements of life. Do you criticize her if she declines to live on her father's scant income (devoting part of her time to doing some unpaid housework in the home), and prefers outside work, independence and greater comfort in living? Even if business means no more to her than these things, is she not exhibiting the general American desire to avoid stagnation and get on? And do you think less of the married woman who works outside the home, when family cares permit, in order to supplement the inadequate earnings of her husband?

Women are making mighty efforts to adjust themselves to the economic changes of the times, and the thinking woman is faced with these facts. More and more women are practically being compelled to enter business because marriage can no longer be regarded as the sole gainful occupation open to women.

Marriage was an excellent investment for a man a few generations ago—all to win and nothing to lose! In those days a woman was an economic asset to a home. The spinning, baking, dairying and soap-making were her jobs, and she added considerably to the store of the household, first in her father's, then in her husband's home. But to-day producing material for the home is acknowledged to be commercial, not domestic business. The modern housekeeper is not a manufacturer, but a home manager. Even if two or more adult women busy themselves with the tasks of the average home, they do not produce increased value in the sense that the woman of a century ago produced. The mother in the household usually does her share and more in return for her support; but the average home can not support another adult woman on a $15 or $20 weekly income, according to modern standards of living. Nevertheless, many fathers are willing to support their daughters at home for a few years until they marry.

Yes, for a few years! But the years that elapse until marriage have steadily lengthened, because rising costs and standards of living have tended to defer marriage for the average man. To-day a wife is quite universally conceded to be more of an expense and less of an investment! Also, with exceeding pride, the modern young man postpones marriage until he can make a home in keeping with his standards. Sometimes indeed he heeds Horace Greeley's counsel: "Young man, don't marry until you're thirty years old; and then you'll not want to!"

These are not pointed out as ideal conditions; they are simply the existing facts which seem to justify in part woman's presence in business.

To answer the questions, Why are women in business; and ought they to be in business. There is not enough work in the home to keep the grown daughters of a household sufficiently occupied. Men of average income do not earn enough to support in idleness grown daughters as well as a wife and younger members of the family. And finally, women can not depend on early marriage to relieve them of the responsibility of self-support.

As a further development of these questions, it may now reasonably be asked: Has the transition from home to business been of benefit to women and to society at large? There can be little doubt that the woman with business experience, whether she has succeeded or not, is usually a more sympathetic, intelligent and companionable individual because of her experience. If she remains unmarried and succeeds in business, is she not in a more self-respecting position than the old-fashioned spinster, without private income, who held the anomalous job of "poor relation" to a tribe of pitying "in-laws"? If she marries, is it not logical to assume that she carries into the home her habit of successful endeavor built on her business experience?

Said ex-President Taft in a newspaper interview: "Every girl should be trained to some occupation which, if followed, will make her independent of marriage as a means of support. Then she need not marry except in obedience to the dictates of her heart. Business makes a woman self-reliant, not a clinging vine. When she marries she can contribute some strength to the partnership. Work and financial dependence are the best possible training for the civic and political responsibilities she may be called upon to assume some day."

WOMAN'S POSITION IN BUSINESS

If business is doing so much in the development of women, why is it that women are still in the subordinate class in business? How can women receive equal recognition with men in the distribution of responsible jobs? (1) By obtaining a better education for business; (2) By adopting a serious interest in work, as men must; (3) By formulating a big, definite purpose for the future.

Certainly there seems some justification for the criticism of women in business when you can observe any day the large number of women in shop or office who are as untrained, indifferent, inefficient and unhappy in their work as the most slipshod housewife, rebellious at the monotony of her tasks. Altho all business women are not to be judged by this type, nevertheless we must recognize that their prevalence in business is bound to color the opinion of men toward women in business.

This is the "ostrich woman" who blinds herself to realities about her work and her future. She feels that to be truly womanly she should look upon business as a temporary occupation to be pursued only until marriage brings a blessed deliverance. As E. S. Martin puts it, "she secretly regards business as an avocation," and joyfully thinks she will soon give up work to be married! With little training, with no work ideals, her business interest begins and ends with her pay envelop. She keeps constantly in evidence her dilettante attitude toward business, thus aiding and abetting the prejudice against women for important posts.

The average young man in business has an ambition for a high executive post, or to own a business some day, and this ambition keeps him interested and progressive. There is no obstacle to our preparing ourselves for as high a post as any of the men with whom we work in friendly rivalry. When we have as definite business ideals as men, there will be less difficulty in obtaining equally high responsibilities and recognition. We will not have to agitate about equal pay. We can command it.

Some one perhaps sighs regretfully, "Ah, but your ideal for a successful business career implies the renunciation of the greater happinesses in a woman's life—home, marriage, motherhood." Why should not marriage, motherhood and home be included in the life program of the business woman as it is in the plans of the business man? She need not sacrifice anything that will enrich life.

"Everywhere we hear that property is sacred, and that life is sacred, but who has said that happiness is sacred?" asks James Mackaye. Surely that happiness is most sacred, most enduring, which is made up of a sane combination of the precious things of life—love, work, human interests—preferably all these, but at least two. A happiness that depends on love alone or work alone is narrowing. Concentrated dependence on one source of happiness drains that source. But where there are several interests, each enriches the other. I can not see that three interests in life instead of one can dwarf a woman's personality; nor that exercise of all her faculties in several kinds of work makes her weaker or "less womanly." There are many women to-day who manage home, family and career simultaneously, and are the better for it both physically and mentally. How she can manage these several interests I have considered in detail in the chapter on "The Business Woman and Marriage."

Even if she is not married, I believe the business woman should have a home of her own, a place that is not only a harmonious haven for her at the end of her day, but where she can exercise her innate instincts for home-building.

Happiness in her chosen work, happiness in her personal life, many interests, participation in movements of public welfare, the stimulus of a worth-while goal, and the development of a self-reliant, joyous personality that stands like a rock through all the vicissitudes of life—this is a vision of the many-sided American business woman. It is at once the reason and the justification of her presence in business.

II

CHOOSING AN OCCUPATION; HOW BUSINESS ANALYZES EMPLOYEES

A SATISFYING occupation is very much like a successful marriage, in this respect: like the permanently happy marriage, it must be built. You can not expect another to make decisions for you in either of these momentous matters. If you elude some of your responsibilities, or depend on some happy accident to bring you good fortune, you are likely to be sorely disappointed in either career. We seem to have some fatalistic idea about both marriage and about occupations. There is an ancient superstition about there being one particular mate somewhere in the world for every individual, and that in due season these two will be drawn together from the mass of humanity in some supernatural fashion! At least, that is what the two believe when they do come together.

A similar idea persists in the minds of very many women—and men too—on the threshold of industrial life. "What is my vocation?" they ask. "Right vocation" has become a fetish, together with a common acceptance of the bromidiom that the majority of people in industry are "square pegs in round holes," and are doomed to remain so by a law of nature. Many intelligent women consider dozens of occupations, in honest doubt as to which particular one is their "vocation," just as if they were born to do some one thing only, and adoption of any other work meant foreordained failure.

We hear very often that a man is a "born artist," or musician, or literary genius; that he has inherited talent, or has shown definite aptitude toward certain work since early youth. But in many cases we find that even these specially "gifted" individuals are able to do more than one thing well. Sarah Bernhardt, in addition to being a great actress, paints well, and has done creditable work in sculpture. The late Dr. S. Weir Mitchell was a noted physician and also an author. Two of our presidents at least, Roosevelt and Wilson, have been able and prolific writers as well as active statesmen. Can we say that they were "born presidents'' only? Colonel Roosevelt has achieved distinction as a hunter of big game, but certainly he was not a "born hunter." As a matter of fact, he was a rather sickly, anemic youth; his later virility was the result of vigorous training and self-development.

It has never been proved that every one is born to one and only one particular calling. Of course it is true that people may be born with an unfitness for certain callings, or may suffer accidents that deprive them of some faculties, and thus the doors to many occupations become closed to them. The individual who is born blind can not expect to be a railroad engineer; the handless person can not be a stenographer.

Barring physical handicaps, almost every line of occupation is open to the normal person, but there must be will and incentive. In certain lines of work you will achieve greater success than in others, no doubt, because you have some native ability or that type of work interests you, and so you have a greater desire to excel therein; or because the rewards are so much larger than in other occupations they stimulate greater endeavor.

Does this mean, then, that you could plunge blindly into any occupation, and by the exercise of will succeed in it? If this is so, why go to any trouble about selecting any one particular calling? Surely, every one has the will to succeed in his occupation—but few do succeed.

If the occupation involved an incentive that spurred you to sustained endeavor, and you kept in action your will to succeed, there is no doubt that you would succeed to the limit of opportunity in that work. But the limit of opportunity in an occupation may not mean success as you understand it because standards of success are interpreted so differently. A bookkeeper may have worked fourteen years in one post, and now earn $25 per week. From her standpoint, she is a success, because she does her work perfectly, and she has attained her ambitions as far as remuneration is concerned. She has succeeded to the limit of opportunity in her work, and she asks no more. She would have applied herself with equal diligence to any other occupation, and would have counted it success when she felt that her work was well done and she was decently paid. But from the standpoint of a more ambitious person, she is in a rut and is a dead failure, because she has recognized a limit of progress, and has no incentive for further effort.

The reason then, for choosing an occupation with care is that one wants to enter a field with an unlimited opportunity. The desire for unlimited opportunity—wealth or power or fame or glory—is what actuates most men who have succeeded. Charles M. Schwab and Andrew Carnegie were not impelled by a vocational call to enter the steel industry. E. H. Harriman was not born with a love for railroads. These men and the hundreds of successful individuals they typify achieved power because power and wealth were their goals and the incentives that spurred them onward. They saw in steel-making and railroad-building unlimited opportunity for power and wealth and they applied themselves diligently to the work they so selected. In other words, they set a goal first, and then proceeded to reach that goal.

Now if you have no ambitions, and do not care particularly for wealth or glory or power or fame, you need not consider at all "what shall be my vocation." Drop into any work, and by exercise of will you will succeed to the limit of its opportunities. But the likelihood is that you really have some aim, some object for which you are in business. Perhaps you want to earn money—much money. Perhaps you desire your daily life to be interesting and therefore you seek an occupation which will give you pleasure while at work. Or you may be ambitious for power—to have control of a business or authority to manage individuals. Or you plan to build a business that will be permanent and secure you an independence for middle age. Or you feel that you would be happiest in some form of social service.

The question is, "what do you expect or desire to get from business?" Once having determined this, your task is to obtain information about the occupations that contain opportunities for your kind of ambition. If you want money, investigate in what lines of work profits are greatest; if you desire power, you must study executive positions and how you can train for them; if you prefer interesting work above money and power, look to the business occupations in which you deal most with the human or mental elements.

Don't be discouraged because you "have no gifts" for the goal you prefer.

There are very few professions in which "native gifts" can be counted the chief requisite, such as a good voice for the operatic or concert stage; inherent taste for painting, sculpture, acting, etc. Even in some of these professions, incentives like environment (parental ambition, artistic atmosphere, etc.) play a large part in influencing the individual toward a certain career. But in the commercial world there are practically no lines of occupation in which facility can not be developed by the normal person. The degree of facility, and the extent of success achieved by different personalities will, of course, vary according to the extent to which each puts will into action.

"What student has not sadly realized the disproportion between his desire to do good work, and the feebleness of his will?" asks Jules Payot, in "The Education of the Will." "Either I have, or I have not, the desire for better things. If I do not have it, all my effort is in vain. To perform a difficult piece of work unwillingly, or not to like what one is trying to attain is to deprive oneself of all chances of success. In order to succeed, one must love his work."

Is this fundamental basis clear? Success in business does not depend on whether you find the one particular occupation which is supposed to be adapted to some innate ability or group of idiosyncrasies which one may possess. It depends on:

(1) What kind of success you wish; that is to say, what goal you would consider success.

(2) Whether you select an occupation in which there is sufficient opportunity for your ambitions.

(3) The incentive which your selected work offers for sustained effort.

(4) The extent to which you apply your will to succeed.

The will to succeed is what helps the ambitious man forward because it conquers so much of the timidity to dare and to risk.

It is what Prof. Walter Dill Scott calls

"love of the game." "For some men," he adds, "buying and selling, or the manufacture of goods, is as great a delight as felling a deer or landing a trout. For such a man enthusiasm for his work is unfailing, and his industry unremittent. A man will develop a love of the game in any business in which he is led to assume a responsibility, to take personal initiative, to feel that he is creating something and that he is expressing himself in his work; and that the work appeals to him as something important and useful."[1]

Now, it is sometimes suggested that the best way to decide on an occupation that will supply an incentive and love of work is to try as many kinds of work as possible. But supposing you try a dozen occupations and still do not experience the thrill of joy in work? There are innumerable chronic experimenters of this kind who are doomed to drifting. Or you might find to your liking a work which was limited in opportunities, that is, a "blind alley" job; or one that did not pay sufficient to support you.

The important thing is, first, to decide

[1] "Increasing Human Efficiency in Business."

on a goal. Know where you are going before you start on your way. Decide whether you want interest or money or power or whether social service is your purpose. Then begin training for that goal. Training may mean a course of study, or a very insignificant post at the bottom of your ladder; it may mean mechanical and monotonous work which you must master by a difficult apprenticeship in order to equip yourself for the high aim you have in mind. What you do immediately at the beginning of your business career is not to be regarded as your life-work, but simply one of the foundation stones of your business structure. Business is the university of life. When you become a copyist in the office, or a "hand" in the shop, or a stock-clerk in the store, you are in your freshman year. Each day's routine is necessary discipline as well as information. But your eyes are focussed on your senior year when your high business goal will be realized.

Assuming that you know nothing of business opportunities, how can you decide on a business aim, and how can you select a beginning occupation? The choice of an industrial occupation is a subject to which a great deal of study has been given in recent years, especially under the title of "vocational guidance." Before deciding on your own method of selecting a beginning occupation, consider what has been done by specialists, students, and business firms who have evolved plans of vocational guidance and selection.

Increased competition, overcrowding of some occupations, and the higher cost of living are the factors which have forced to the foreground a need for premeditated selection of work rather than haphazard dropping into any calling, with neither desire nor interest in the work. Young people learn that there are occupations which are overcrowded and they wish to avoid such occupations. They also have ambitions for better living and for personal progress. What avenues of employment shall they enter? Many school teachers have been forced to act as guides in the selection of work, because the student faced the need of earning a livelihood and her studies had not equipped her for any specific line of industry.

Simultaneously, business recognized that it was greatly handicapped by inefficient workers in industry. Some firms sought to remedy the condition by installing schools and providing various educational facilities to employees. But others attacked the problem from the beginning, by applying tests to applicants, and eliminating those who disclosed unfitness under such tests.

For example, take a large corporation employing hundreds of clerks. For years they suffered considerable loss because of the large number of clerks who were engaged and trained for a few months, but then found incompetent, and were dismissed. These employees were engaged after a preliminary interview, or after an examination of a letter of application — neither of which methods contained any dependable basis for judging adaptability to the work.

Then a psychologist was called in, and after about one year's work, and studying the needs of the organization, he formulated a set of tests for applicants that proved exceedingly valuable. They consisted of about twenty-four pages of examination questions, and the time for answering them was limited. These sheets contained carefully worked out tests for mathematical ability, eyesight, intelligence, knowledge of simple facts about geography, etymology, color, etc.—a species of Binet-Simon tests for adults. On the quickness, accuracy and intelligence of the replies, the applicant's fitness was determined. As the tests have been used only for a few years, it can not be said positively that they are infallible. The fact remains, nevertheless, that even in the short period in which they have been in operation, there has been a great decrease in the percentage of necessary dismissals for incompetency, and that a higher intelligence in the clerical staff prevails.

Here is another method of analysis in force in a large advertising agency. The accompanying chart, No. 1, is filled in by both employees, who give an estimate of themselves, and by executives, both being considered when judging the efficiency of an employee. If an employee is retained, she is asked to mark this chart again a year or two later, and the comparison of progress made, or the advance or decline in ability is exceedingly helpful. This can not, of course, be accepted as a scientifically accurate method of judging fitness. It is simply one of the means used to record observations of employees as a basis for forming judgment.

Chart No. 2 is a similar method for helping to classify employees according to their efficiency and equipment for promotion, and has been used with success.

Some very interesting psychological tests were made by Prof. Walter Dill Scott in selecting salesmen. This is a particularly difficult class of employees to test for fitness, and also a class on which business executives spend a great deal of money in futile experiments. Salesmen are engaged usually on the strength of superficial impressions. Giving a salesman a "try-out" of a few weeks is an expensive process. Professor Scott applied a series of tests for salesmen based on these factors: (1) the standard of medical examination; (2) the standard of the educational minimum; (3) the standard of native ability; (4) the standard of relative rank and position.

On Chart 3 are shown some of the examination questions which were applied to

(NO. 1)—SELF-ANALYSIS CHART FOR EMPLOYEES

Mark on basis of 100% Perfect

10	20	30	40	50	60	70	80	90	100	
										Age
										Health
										Height
										Weight
										Strength
										Endurance
										Appearance
										Suppleness
										Observation
										Concentration
										Thought Speed
										Seeing Likenesses
										Seeing Differences
										Tact
										Culture
										Memory
										Imagination
										General Education
										Analytical Ability
										Experience in Adv.-
										Mech. Tendency
										Artistic Tendency
										Literary Tendency
										Initiative
										Decision
										Industry
										Thoroughness
										Carefulness
										Order
										Sense of Responsibility
										Personality
										Intuition
										Enthusiasm
										Cheerfulness
										Sympathy
										Loyalty
										Honesty
										Morals and Sobriety
										Truthfulness
										Self Confidence
										Justice
										Patience

(No. 2)—LAKE PLACID CLUB GRADE CARD

The purpose of this card is to discover and promote unusual efficiency. Mark each number on scale of 5: 1 eliminate, 2 doubtful, 3 common, 4 better, 5 best.

HEALTH				
1 Energy, endurance, strength				
PERSONALITY				
2 Ambition, ideals, will				
3 Cheerful, good disposition				
4 Courteous, good manners, quiet				
MENTAL QUALIFICATIONS				
5 Aptitude, intelligence				
6 Accuracy, attention, good memory				
7 Interest, teachable, willing				
8 Neat in work, dress, person				
9 Prompt, punctual				
10 Order, system				
CHARACTER, CONDUCT, ETHICS				
MEN 11 Use of liquor and tobacco				
MEN 12 Profanity and vulgarity				
MEN 13 Conduct toward women				
WOMEN 11 Lunching				
WOMEN 12 Conduct toward men				
13 Late hours out or indoors				
14 Honest, truthful				
15 Loafing, shirking				
16 WASTE, misuse of equipment or food				
17 Acceptance of TIPS				
18 Cooperation, loyalty				
19 Quality of work				
20 Quantity of work				
Total per cent.				
TRAITS FOR SPECIAL PROMOTION				
X 1 Executive: grasp of details, responsible				
X 2 Initiative, resourceful				
X 3 Discipline, control, tact				
X 4 Judgment, sense of proportion				
X 5 Fairness, justice (no favoritism)				
Multiply by 4 to give per cent.				
Total X per cent.				

$1 is offered for each new suggestion, submitted in writing and finally adopted, which will improve service or lessen cost. $10 will be paid for the most suggestions, above 5, submitted by one person and adopted. Cooperation of all employees is cordially invited.

show the second and third factor. The standard of physique and the standard of intelligence are fairly determinable by the application of physical and psychological tests. But, as a supplementary basis for judging the possible fitness of a man for a sales position, another plan was adopted. There were twenty-nine applicants that had to be interviewed. Each of the eight sales managers of the company, in a separate room, interviewed separately each of the twenty-nine applicants, and recorded in writing the place he would assign to each one on the list. Most of these sales managers had been employing salesmen for many years, but their decisions were governed by indefinite influences—intuition or some vague superficial impression. After all the applicants had been interviewed, a table was prepared showing the place assigned to each applicant on the list by the various sales managers, also the position the men were assigned according to their examination results. The differences of opinion among the sales managers was enormous. One placed applicant M 1st on the list; another placed him 26th; another selected applicant F as

(No. 3)—SOME OF THE EXAMINATION QUESTIONS IN PSYCHOLOGICAL TESTS FOR SALESMEN[2]

Read the general directions before you do anything else.
General Directions:

Do what the printed instructions tell you to do.

Do not ask the examiner any questions about the examination.

Do not ask any other person who is taking the examination any question or watch any one to see what he or she does.

Work as rapidly as you can *without making any mistakes.*

If you do make a mistake, correct it neatly.

Do 1 first, then 2, then 3, and so on.

I. Write your name and permanent address here.

....

....

Instructions for 2, 3 and 4:

After each word printed below you are to write some word, according to the further directions. Write plainly, but as quickly as you can. If you can not think of the right word in about 3 seconds *go ahead to the next.*

II. Write the *opposites* of the words in this column, as shown in the first three.

number here.................... Show by a cross when the nights are longer: in summer?" ....in winter? .... Give the correct answer to this question: "Does water run uphill?"................and repeat your answer here................ Do nothing here (5 + 7 =........), unless you skipped the preceding question; but write the first letter of your first name and the last letter of your last name at the ends of this line:....................

X. Place in the bracket preceding each English proverb the number of the African proverb to which the English proverb corresponds in meaning.

ENGLISH PROVERBS

(   ) Married in haste, we repent at leisure.
(   ) Answer a fool according to his folly.
(   ) One swallow does not make a summer.
(   ) First catch your hare.
(   ) Adding insult to injury.
(   ) Curses come home to roost.
(   ) Distance lends enchantment to the view.
(   ) We can all endure the misfortunes of others.

AFRICAN PROVERBS

1. One tree does not make a forest.
2. "I nearly killed the bird." No one can eat "nearly" in a stew.
3. Full-belly child says to hungry-belly child, "Keep good cheer."
4. Distant firewood is good firewood.

good—*bad*	far—
day—*night*	up—
up—*down*	smooth—
long—	early—
soft—	dead—
white—	hot—

asleep—

* * * * * * *

IX. Do what it says to do as quickly as you can, but be careful to notice just what it does say.

With your pencil make a dot over any one of these letters, *F G H I J*, and a comma after the longest of these three words: *boy, mother, girl*. Then, if Christmas comes in March, make a cross right here................, but if not, pass along to the next question and tell where the sun rises.................... If you believe that Edison discovered America, cross out what you just wrote, but if it was someone else, put in a number to complete this sentence: "A horse has....................feet." Write *yes*, no matter whether China is in Africa or not....................; and then give a wrong answer to this question: "How many days are there in the week?" ....Write any letter except *g* just after this comma, and then write *no* if 2 times 5 are 10.................... Now, if Tuesday came after Monday, make two crosses here; but if not, make a circle here....................or else a square here.................... Be sure to make three crosses between these two names of boys: George.................... Henry. Notice these two numbers: 3, 5. If iron is heavier than water, write the larger number here .... But if iron is lighter write the smaller

5. Ashes fly in the face of him who throws them.
6. If the boy says he wants to tie the water with a string, ask him whether he means the water in the pot or the water in the lagoon.
7. The ground-pig said: "I do not feel so angry with the man who killed me as with the man who dashed me on the ground afterward."
8. Quick loving a woman means quick not loving a woman.

Just as soon as you finish, give your paper to the examiner so as to get credit for having completed the work before time was called.

The most brilliant adult applicants complete the ten parts of this Test in about fourteen minutes. An intelligence that enables the possessor to complete the ten parts in thirty-three minutes, with a total of eighteen errors, is assumed to be sufficient for the applicants for selling positions for one organization. The applicants for another organization must attain a much higher standard, which is a limit of twenty minutes and not more than eight errors. In these two organizations the applicants who fail to attain the standard accomplishment in Test I, are rejected unless in some other intelligence tests the minimum standards of accomplishments are surpassed. No person of a low degree of intelligence can complete Test I accurately in thirty minutes. Occasionally a person of good native ability and with a common school education or better fails to complete some one of the intelligence tests accurately and quickly. By the use of several different kinds of tests for native ability there is but little danger of rejecting a worthy applicant.

[2] From "Advertising and Selling," October, 1915.

the best, while two others placed him 24th. The only unanimous decision was as to the 28th man on the list—all agreed he was the poorest applicant. But two months after the men were put to work, the four men who stood highest in actual results were men who had not been given first place by any of the interviewers. In fact, the star salesman had been placed 20th on the list by one interviewer.

This is no reflection on the perception of the managers who interviewed the men. This is exactly what happens in actual practise in most organizations—that men who seem doubtful material when engaged develop well; while men who appear to be "skyrocket" producers when interviewed, fall flat after a few weeks' trial. Any unstandardized method of selection, a dependence on intuition alone, is bound to be faulty.

Chart 4 shows another instance where 26 employees were interviewed by five managers, and subjected to psychological tests. This list was prepared finally to show the place assigned each individual by the managers, according to the psychological test and then

(No. 4)—RATING OF EMPLOYES ACCORDING TO MANAGERS' JUDGMENT, PSYCHOLOGICAL TEST, COMPARED WITH ACTUAL FIRST RANK—(*Prof. Walter Dill Scott tests.*)

	Firm Rank	Test Rank	Boss's Judgment: Boss A	Boss B	Boss C	Boss D	Boss E
Employee A	1	2.5	1	1	1	1	..
" B	2	6	3	3	4	2	..
" C	3	4	8	2	3	3	3
" D	4	2.5	5	5	6	5	1
" E	5	5	6	7	5	12	5
" F	6	7	7.5	4	2	6	7
" G	7	1	2	6	10	8	11
" H	8	15	12	8	9	..	..
" I	9	9	10	16	8	9	..
" J	10	19	9	10	7	18	..
" K	11.5	14	7	14	14	17	..
" L	11.5	10	4	19	15	14	..
" M	13	13	13	12	12	21	9
" N	14	8	11	13	17	..	..
" O	15	12	19	9	11	15	21
" P	16	11	14	11	..	11	25
" Q	17	18	15	18	16	..	..
" R	18	16	20	15	18	..	19
S	19	22	16	22	20	..	15
" T	20	21	22	23	24	20	13
" U	21	24	24	17	19	26	..
" V	22	17	23	20	25	23	17
" W	23	25	17.5	25	23	..	..
" X	24	20	21	21	22	24	23
" Y	25	23	26	24	21	..	..
" Z	26	26	25	26	26	25	..
Correlation of Firm Rank and Test Rank	..	.884	..	..	..	..	..
Correlation with Test Rank	..	..	.804	.878	.814	.911	.571
Correlation with Boss D	..	.911	.777	.863	.877	..	.646
Correlation with Boss A	..	.804	..	.704	.754	..	..

the actual firm rank of each employee, which shows how far right each manager and also the psychologists were.

Most of these tests are intended for use to pick people for jobs, and to keep out the unfit. Business houses are discovering that it pays to formulate tests and special analyses to keep out the incompetent. They can afford to spend thousands of dollars in order to get the right people.

But the great problem to consider now is, how to pick jobs for people—how to determine on a goal and a beginning occupation. In recent years a class of "vocational guides" has grown up—men and women who undertake to analyze you and tell you what you ought to do. Some of these counsellors have helped business houses tremendously by applying their systems of selecting employees, but this, of course, is the elimination system. One such specialist classifies all individuals under the following heads, and makes general recommendations for employment on these factors: (a) Physically strong, *vs.* physically weak; (b) Mentally strong; (c) Manual workers; (d) Settled *vs.* roving temperament; (e) Indoor *vs.* outdoor worker; (f) Directive *vs.* dependent employee; (g) Originality *vs.* imitativeness; (h) Detail *vs.* large-plan thinking; (i) Adaptability *vs.* obstinacy; (j) Active or plan habits.

Dr. Katherine M. H. Blackford, who is known for her studies of individuals according to their achievements, bases her conclusions of ability on cranial and facial contour. In the selection of applicants, the Blackford plan is claimed to be successful, as it endeavors to eliminate the possible unfit and to lessen the experimenting and expensive training of employees. But we can not throw the responsibility of selecting an aim in life on a blanket system, the conclusions of which are not based on an intimate study of every new individual separately.

You can not thrust the responsibility of selecting an aim for you on an outsider. Only a god, or a magician, could know, in a few hours, everything about your character, ambitions, and secret aspirations. But you yourself can decide what aim is best for you, and in selecting it you can use some of the same methods which business houses have used in selecting employees—

the method of elimination. Eliminate from the list of possible occupations those in which you are definitely not interested. If you have no taste for mathematics, do not condemn yourself to office drudgery, because without love for the work, you will not succeed. It does not matter that office work may be more "refined" than some form of manual labor in which you are more interested. Without *will* for its tasks you can not make progress.

But it happens very often that the individual honestly does not know what business aim will interest her. Then the best method of analysis for use in deciding is self-analysis. Chart 5 shows one plan of averaging personal ability and tendencies which may indicate a business aim that will enlist your interest.

Chart 6 is a summary of abilities required for a high-class stenographer. This is a "beginning occupation" which opens up a large business career to the determined woman sufficiently interested in work to cultivate her abilities.

A great deal of valuable information on occupations is distributed by organizations

(No. 5)—SELF-ANALYSIS CHART TO SUGGEST A BUSINESS AIM

Characteristics	*Corresponding Aim*	*Beginning Occupation*
Dynamic Original Progressive Large scope Imaginative	Creative work: Advertising, Selling, Business management, Higher executive work	Clerical Work
Mathematical tastes Grasp of detail Concentration	Office management, Higher accounting	Clerical Work
Aggressiveness Social temperament Adaptability Persistence Agreeable personality	Selling occupations, Ownership or Management of store	In retail store or canvassing
Manual tastes Physical coordination Practical viewpoint Patience	Manufacturing ownership	Factory occupations

(No. 6)—STENOGRAPHERS' SELF-ANALYSIS CHART

Marks: 1 point—Poor and improvement unlikely
2 " —Poor, but may improve
3 " —Fair
4 " —Good
5 " —Exceptionally good

Education

Marks: 1 point—Less than grade
2 " —Finished grades
3 " —Business school
4 " —High school
5 " —College

(1) PHYSICAL QUALITIES — POINTS

Hearing ....
Eyesight ....
Nerve control ....
Endurance ....
General health ....

(2) MENTAL CHARACTERISTICS

Memory ....
Concentration ....
Reliability ....
Accuracy ....
Persistence ....
Initiative ....
Imagination ....
Ambition ....
Industry ....

(3) EDUCATIONAL ASSETS

Stenographic speed..............................
Typewriting speed..............................
What education..............................
Well-read ....
Languages known (how many)..............................
Command of English..............................
Spelling ....
Punctuation ....

(4) PERSONAL HABITS AND CHARACTER

Promptness ....
Dress and personal appearance..............................
Poise in manner..............................
Loyalty ....
Business honor..............................
Tact and good temper..............................
Ability to cooperate..............................

Average ———

like the National Association of Corporation Schools, New York, the National Educational Association of Washington, D. C., the Women's Educational and Industrial Union, of Boston; and an excellent bulletin was published in February, 1914, by the Pedagogical Library of the Philadelphia Board of Education, called "A Working Library on Vocational Guidance and Education." In many cities there are vocational guidance bureaus which have available information on occupations and their opportunities.

Then secure information about local opportunities in the line of work for which you have some ambitions. Your first step is to get as complete information as possible about the occupation in which you are interested—what preparatory education or apprenticeship is necessary, what are the requirements, what are the opportunities and limitations. Then begin as early as possible to get practical training for the work, supplemented by study, and keep on studying after you have begun actual work. The greatest stimulus to progress in any work is continued study and research in the field.

"But I don't know what I want to do," is a frequent remark made by women who know only that they must work, but feel no special leaning in any one direction. The responsibility of selecting a lucrative and pleasant work is offered to a teacher, or a vocational guidance expert, with the expectation that one of these authorities possesses the power to discern hidden genius and suggest immediately a fitting occupation. It is not the function of the vocational guide to select one particular kind of work fitted to a particular individual, with the assurance that this vocation, and this one only, will lead to ultimate success. It is unreasonable to expect such service. The responsibility of selection lies with you. The vocational authority can only supply trustworthy data on the requirements and opportunities in the field which interests you.

If you do not know what you want to do, if all branches of business appeal to you equally, and you feel no special inclination or ability for selling, or mathematics, or clerical occupations, analyze your aims in life, and find out what you expect to secure from a business career. If your aim is to own a business, you can enter an occupation which will train you for such a goal. If your aim is to earn as much money as possible, obtain information about the occupations which offer the highest pay, and get training for some such occupation.

It rarely happens that an adult has not some special ability or inclination, but it does happen with children who have to earn their livelihood before they have developed any aptitudes and have had little or no opportunity to know themselves and to know what they like. It is for this reason that the type of curriculum in elementary schools such as is typified by the Gary system, is valuable, because it provides for exercise of many faculties of the child until she knows what work she looks forward to with glee, and what work she dislikes.

Know what work you like, and even if it is only a faint indication of ability, it will prove a tiny light in the dark which will lead you to an eventual goal. For you will succeed only as you "love the game." If you have no particular talent, then throw yourself heart and soul into any work upon which you have decided; fall in love with it deliberately, and consciously, and it will bring success, and what is greater, happiness in work and in daily life.

Eventually we may develop in this country some central bureau of vocational guidance where will be recorded all the information necessary regarding all occupations, and where the records of business, the information developed by psychologists, and the facilities of a national employment bureau will be available to every occupation-seeker. There are so many variations in industry, so many changes from day to day, that the only trustworthy data is that which is continually revised and kept up-to-date. The following sources are sorely needed to-day by a large number of men and women in, or about to enter into industry:

(1) A Central Bureau of Information on Occupations.

> This would be really a library where records of industrial and professional occupations are kept up-to-date and complete, through information and cooperation of business interests and educational institutions and agencies.

(2) A Psychological and Physiological Laboratory.[3]

Here individuals could be tested to determine relative ability in any particular work. Psychological tests for specific pieces of work are being developed from time to time—like standards for stenographers or typists, telephone operators, inspector of bicycle balls, salesmen, etc. This might not only supply a suggestion for an occupation, but also is an index of relative efficiency. Mary L's grade, upon psychological test, is so-and-so; and she presents this record as a dependable gage to her worth. Her remuneration then, is not what she can influence her employer to pay by her ability to sell her services, but with a recognized basis for testing relative efficiency of workers, there will also be a basis for formulating rcognized standards of remuneration.

(3) National and Municipal Employment Bureaus.

One of our greatest inefficiencies is the lack of organized information regarding employ-

[3] As this goes to press work is being begun by the Economic Psychology Association, New York, along such lines. This organization, composed of six foremost psychologists in America, collaborating with business men, conducts investigations and tests to establish standards for employment.

ment needs. There is a dearth of workers at one place, and a dearth of employment at another. Information is scattered, and many women and men who would go anywhere for work do not know where to seek it. A National Employment Bureau, cooperating with Municipal Employment Bureaus in every sizable city in the union—and also with farm districts—could do much to relieve the unemployment problem by acting as a clearing house for the equal distribution of labor.

III

HOW TO MARKET YOUR ABILITY

ONCE a man tried to sell me some insurance. He called on the last day of the month, produced a pound packet of statistics from his pocket, and began to quote endless rows of figures to prove the superiority of his company over its competitors. He dwelt on the millions of dollars of assets, the millions paid in dividends, and the number of men and women for whom he had written hundred thousand dollar policies, until I felt that my paltry few thousand dollars of insurance would be a mere decimal point in all this wealth. As a climax to this solicitation, he suggested that I fill my application immediately in order that he could include the policy in his month's business as the monthly sales contest closed that day! Some months later another enterprising life insurance solicitor called. But instead of starting with the story of his company, he concentrated on the advantages that would accrue to me through an investment in the policy he offered. Statistics about his company were shown merely as proof of its ability to fulfil the obligations it assumed toward me. He made me feel that I was not spending money, but exchanging values, and exchanging them at a profit.

Therein lies one element of good salesmanship, and it holds true whether you are selling merchandise, or insurance, or personal ability. As soon as the buyer is shown that he is exchanging values at a profit to himself, the transaction succeeds.

Every business woman will find it exceedingly helpful to be familiar with the elements of good salesmanship, for so many business problems can be solved by applying selling principles. The very first problem confronting a woman trained for business is a sales problem—how to sell her own services. Applying for a job is simply seeking a desirable buyer for your time and labor. You are in the same position toward your possible employer as that employer is to the public to whom he wishes to sell his wares. Let us follow the steps of the successful seller of merchandise, and see how you can adopt his methods in selling your services.

He spends months or years, and large sums of money in preparing an article that the public will want. Then the article is drest in an attractive package so that it will impress favorably possible customers. Is that not your first step too—making your services desirable? But, like the manufacturer, you too have competition, and you too require features of superiority in your services if you are to overcome competition. To make your equipment clear to yourself, write a list of your marketable assets: (a) Extent of training and education; (b) Skill at work, average or superior and why; (c) What supplementary abilities render your services especially valuable; (d) Your past experience and what it has taught you; (e) Does your personality influence a favorable impression; or can your dress, manners, speech, poise, gait, etc., be improved?

The second step of the manufacturer is to analyze the market. He reads trade papers, books on his industry, learns through personal investigation, or trustworthy reports of others what are the conditions of the market. He studies competitive products to learn why some succeed and others fail. Now that you have a clear idea of your equipment, study the fields where you may be able to sell your services best. If your expertness at work distinguishes you from the mass of competitors, your search for a job can be confined only to those places where the highest skill is required. An extremely rapid stenographer who contented herself with a job where she had only a dozen letters a day to write, but was paid a good salary, found very soon that she had not sold her services well, because she was in a blind alley, as far as advancement was concerned. Remember this, in studying a market for your services: (a) aim high—for the highest, most responsible post you believe you can fill; (b) know the opportunities and demands of many commercial fields in order that you may have a wide range of choice; (c) try to select an industry in which your supplementary abilities may be valuable. You will probably not obtain as high a post as you aim for, but that spirit will keep you away from "blind alley" jobs.

The stimulation of a high aim will keep you preparing for the bigger posts and as soon as you are equipped to shoulder the responsibility you will have little trouble in obtaining it.

Many inexperienced business women make the mistake of excluding from their interest all occupations except the particular one in which they are engaged. A well-equipped business woman knows something about all branches of commerce. She may be an office woman, but she reads, and thinks and keeps herself informed about the business of selling, of conditions in some one or more manufacturing fields which may interest her, and about financial matters. Why should this be necessary? Because, the more she knows of all business, the wider is the field in which to sell her own services. When she knows the demands of a number of industries, she is able to select the one in which her particular group of abilities can be sold to the best advantage. Moreover, if industrial changes, or a physical handicap, make it impossible for her to continue at the work for which she was trained, she is not wholly at sea regarding a new source of livelihood.

Supplementary abilities like a knowledge of music, of color or line, a taste for mathematics, writing ability, etc., may sometimes be used as a guide in selecting a market for your services. Here is a woman who for some years earned her living writing advertisements, and who, possessing especially good taste in furnishings, sought work in that particular field. This ability was only supplementary to her skill in commercial writing, yet it gave her a definite advantage over competitors.

Supplementary abilities are very often a key to a larger opportunity than could be obtained even by extreme proficiency in the work attendant upon a particular post. This advertising writer, for example, developed into a much greater success as an interior decorator. A stenographer, with a knowledge of French and Spanish, created for herself a much more important position as foreign correspondent. Your supplementary abilities, even if they are very extraneous to your work as you have been trained for it, should be considered carefully when you study the fields where your services can be sold best.

The third step of the manufacturer is how to sell his goods and keep them sold. The best automobile, the most beautiful piano, the superior quality of clothes, are not sought out of their obscurity by eager buyers. There is too much competition. The business man, therefore, uses aggressive sales and advertising methods to present his wares in their most favorable light to attract purchasers Even after his goods are sold he must keep on advertising, improving his product, offering better service, so as to maintain his good reputation and increase his sales.

It is just as important to know how to sell your services well as to have services to sell. Indeed, there are women who know the art of selling so well that they are able to obtain far better positions for themselves than women with more ability in work, but less selling ability. It is not an especially commendable achievement merely to "get a job"—any kind of a job. You do yourself an injustice if you fail to get the best possible opportunity for your group of abilities. Poor and unjustifiable sales often undermine a merchant's business—cut-price sales, sales to dealers who have not the trade for that high type of merchandise. These are "sales that do not stay sold." The job that is unsuited to your powers, or below your capacity is a "poor sale." If you get the job only because you offer to work for a lower salary than competitors, it is a "cheap sale" and will not stay sold, for the market is full of underbidders. The only safe competition is the competition based on quality and service—not on cheapness.

If there is a lively demand for your kind of work, one of the following methods will probably secure a position for you. But if, because of an over-glutting of the market, hard times, or other conditions, you find your search difficult, it is best to use all possible methods simultaneously. Better take the risk of having several positions offered from two or three sources, than to spin out the weeks of waiting while you try each method in turn: (1) Insert an advertisement in newspapers; (2) Insert an advertisement in the trade papers of the industry in which you have had experience; (3) Answer published advertisements by letter, telephone, or in person; (4) Send out circular letters to a carefully selected list of firms for whom you would like to work, either because of your particular experience, supplementary abilities, or the wide opportunities in their organizations; (5) Create a new post; (6) Employ a reliable agency.

An advertisement must be attractive, direct, and convincing in order to produce results. In a praiseworthy effort to be original, men and women sometimes prepare ludicrous advertisements. Originality does not mean eccentricity.

Before writing an advertisement for a position, get a text-book on advertising and read the pages or chapters which give information on the writing of advertisements, or "copy," as it is called. If you can not do this yourself, it is much better to enlist the aid of some one familiar with the preparation of advertisements. It will add to the cost, but also to the effectiveness of your announcement.

When answering an advertisement in person, be prepared to give full information about your education, experience, special ability, and temperament. If you are quick and observing, you can speak of your experience, education, etc., in relation to the job you are applying for, as you go along. In other words, you will offer your wares from the buyer's view-point, and your services will seem a desirable and profitable investment, rather than an expense to be debated over.

Some women are so nervous in a personal interview that they fail to carry conviction. They are ill at ease, do not give adequate information about themselves, and an unexpected question scatters all their ideas to the winds. After it is over they remember the good things they might have said, and are filled with self-reproach for the opportunity lost. So it is sometimes wise to have prepared a written statement of education, experience, qualifications for the post, special abilities, etc., and this can be shown at an opportune moment during the interview, if it seems necessary.

Be brief, specific, but not monosyllabic, and do not drag in unnecessary details. Emphasize the affirmative side of your experience, but be honest about your limitations. If you are asked your reasons for leaving a former position, do not swerve into a long and dreary narrative full of criticisms of your previous employer's business. When all is said, make a start to go before it becomes necessary for your prospective employer to suggest that the interview is closed. This hastens the decision and sometimes it influences a more favorable one than if you drag the interview.

Incidentally, be sure that your clothes are businesslike and neat before you personally apply for a position. Not only will your clothes influence opinion about your personality, but they affect your own mental attitude and poise. Don't wear your "best clothes" or any finery. It may make you feel self-conscious, and also is likely to give your interviewer a false idea of the degree of your prosperity!

Use the rules of successful advertising in applying for a job by letter: (1) Attract attention by a striking and unusual opening; (2) Arouse interest by stating concrete facts important to the reader; (3) Create a demand for your services by describing attractively the qualities which you possess and which you know are desired; (4) Suggest action by a specific request at the close.

Letters that contain such ancient phrases as the following have no power to hold the reader: "In answer to your advertisement, I beg to apply for the position, and am enclosing some letters of recommendations," etc.; "I am rapid and accurate"; "A trial will demonstrate my ability." These sentences are trite, meaningless and are dull and unconvincing.

The modern business man is interested in definite statements of what you have done and what you can do for him. The old phrases have worn smooth through unceasing use; they slide through the mind without leaving an impression. Express yourself in simple, vigorous language without these "bromidioms" and your letter will grip the mind.

Tell your story briefly, but with facts and instances instead of adjectives and generalizations. Thus: "My daily average was 50 dictated letters and less than 2 per cent. of errors," wrote an alert young stenographer. "I have an idea that may help increase your sales," was the opening sentence in an application for a clerkship in the sales department of a manufacturer. Of course, every business man is willing to listen to any one who has an idea for enlarging his sales totals! "I helped evolve a collection scheme that cut down our bad accounts 30 per cent. last year," wrote an applicant for a post in an instalment house.

Business is forever alert to employ people who can help increase sales, reduce expenses, or raise the efficiency of office or shop. You have some helpful quality that can be developed for business use, and if you present it attractively you will have an interested listener or reader.

Do not place too much trust in the "letter of recommendation" as an open sesame to a good position. There was a time when an applicant was expected to produce a sheaf of testimonials from previous employers, from schools, teachers, pastor, from almost everybody except ancestors. But because these letters were given so freely, business men had less and less faith in the generous "recommendation" given to a departing employee. To-day it is not the saccharine letter of recommendation, not the "pull" of social or political relations that secures and holds a post for you, but your own personality, supported by recognizable ability. There is a definite rule against nepotism in the most advanced types of organizations; and in some cases sisters are not permitted to work in the same department because of its possible interference with discipline.

The woman who has had unusual experience, or has a special ability sometimes finds her best opportunity after having circularized a carefully prepared list—perhaps one she compiled herself.

Here is a woman who has handled the complaints for a mail-order house. Would she get quick results if she waited to see an advertisement for just such a post as she wanted? Hardly. She makes a list of all the firms likely to require such services—mail-order, department store, credit and instalment houses, etc., in her own and nearby cities to which she would willingly go, and she sends a snappy, well-written form letter to every name on the list.

Or, here is a woman who has sold real estate. She copies from the city directory the names of real estate firms she would like to work for; or perhaps she desires to use her experience in another field, like the selling of stocks and bonds, or pianos or other objects in which the investment is large. Or here is some one who has managed her own retail business and is capable of assuming a similar responsibility in another establishment. A stenographer with several years' experience in the automobile business has knowledge which would make her more valuable to an automobile firm than to some other business. In each case, a circular is sent to a good list of local firms in such lines as interest her.

If letters are ignored, or there is a courteous reply expressing regret at the "lack of opportunity at present," a follow-up should be used, perhaps ten days after the first letter. Your letter of last week may have come at the wrong time to get attention, or there may have been a change in the organization in the meantime which may affect you favorably. If the two letters fail, make a personal call, just as a salesman would if he were soliciting business and his "prospects" evinced no interest in his letters. A personal call may dispel indifference, and leave a definite impression of your individuality which is more likely to be remembered than a letter of application on file. Whatever is good selling practise is good job-getting practise. There are a few other details to be observed when making application:

(1) In writing, never use social or monogrammed stationery. Use plain white sheets, typewritten with pen signature, unless the position applied for demands good penmanship in which case the letter should be written.

(2) State facts briefly, if possible in tabular form so as to make easy reading.

(3) Don't leave it to your prospective employer to make the appointment. "Can I see you Tuesday morning at 9:30?" is more likely to result in an interview than "When may I call to demonstrate my ability?"

(4) Again, and most important: have something definite to offer—something "out of the rut." Avoid the platitudinous boast, but fill your application with specific, illuminating and simply phrased instances.

(5) Send a special delivery or registered letter if you are applying for some post of unusual importance or which you are specially desirous of securing.

It is comparatively easy to get a job when you have most of the equipment that business demands. But supposing you are handicapped, either by a physical condition like poor sight or poor hearing, or age, or inexperience, or inadequate education? What then? This is a frequent question, especially from middle-aged business women who have lost a good job which they held for many years and are hopeless about getting another.

But the same rules about job-getting apply. No matter what are the minor handicaps, every individual has some quality of value. That quality is the thing on which to concentrate and to become perfect; to find or create a place for it, and to present it with fine salesmanship. But the handicap is to be kept in the background of the mind. Dr. Felix Adler once offered this maxim as a helpful principle in life, and it applies with tremendous force to this particular problem. Said he, "Keep paramount the things which are paramount, and subordinate the things which are subordinate."

I have received hundreds of letters from middle-aged business women who were panic-stricken because they had met some prejudice against them on account of their age. Because age is an ineradicable objection, they were obsessed with fear until they saw only their handicap. But handicaps are the "subordinate things." The "paramount things" are the good, constructive qualities of mind and experience, and there is always a place for them. If the middle-aged woman is cut off from ordinary opportunities, she can create new ones, and if she has been the thinking type of business woman, interested in industries outside of her own immediate work, she will not be dismayed at the prospect.

As a matter of fact, there are many jobs, small and large, where middle age is a definite asset, where dignity and experience are given the preference over youth, such as that of reception clerk, matron in charge of a lunch-room, or of a rest-room in a large organization, or that of welfare secretary, a post especially suitable for a mature woman who has qualifications for the work. Then there are outside jobs of selling, investigating, demonstrating, where a woman must be mature in order to create confidence.

Even the handicaps of poor sight, poor hearing, etc., are not insurmountable. A young stenographer was utterly discouraged because her eyes gave her so much trouble. But she lessened the strain when she used the dictating machine and the "touch type-writing" system. Handicaps like weakened health, unattractive personality are all remediable. If the difficulty is lack of experience and there is no other way open, then some experience can be obtained by offering to work for a time for a nominal, or no salary. Indeed, in some foreign countries the inexperienced young clerk actually has had to pay a business firm to let him acquire practise in commercial routine.

If the physique becomes weakened, the safest procedure is to change the occupation immediately. Many office women are anemic and spiritless after many years of indoor work and easily become despondent if they have to change positions. But sometimes an entire change of work puts them "on the map" again. One office woman regained health by doing rough, outdoor work for a year; another spent two years doing housework. But both came back to their office jobs physically stronger and with a more cheerful outlook on life.

Even an unattractive personality can be made agreeable by immaculateness of person and better apparel. The manager of a large employment agency once confest that he did not have the courage to tell some of the capable women who could not obtain positions that it was only because of their unpleasant personality. Women are extremely sensitive on this point. It is of fundamental importance that the business woman shall look well when she applies for a job. Indeed, here the woman with a handicap has an advantage over the handicapped man, for the possibilities of women's apparel lend themselves to covering a multitude of sins.

When trying to sell your services, remember that there is only a market for good qualities. Lead your constructive, desirable qualities to the foreground. Your handicaps are to be mentioned honestly, but lightly, and kept subordinate, even in your own mind.

IV

WHAT DO EMPLOYERS PAY?

When we speak of "salary" we refer to the most unstandardized of all modes of payment. Skilled workers in factories, unskilled laborers in almost every field have wage standards established by market conditions in their locality or by labor unions. A good carpenter gets his $4 a day, no matter for whom he works. But you can find a bookkeeper who is worth $30 a week working for $15. Or, as O. Henry once put it, "she received $7 a week of what she earned."

Why is this so? It is curious but true that the mental labor market is the one least organized to cope with the compensation problem. There are comparatively few office workers' unions. There are no recognized, dependable wage standards for various jobs, nor for varying efficiency in such jobs. The salary of the office worker both in detail and in executive posts depends considerably on her ability to sell her services well, partly on arbitrary compensation standards of an individual firm, which do not provide a margin for special experience or ability.

This lack of standardized salaries for mental labor is at the bottom of discontent with remuneration. The woman who is well equipped for her job, but has no ability to sell her own services, is likely to be poorly paid, because she has not the sustaining compulsion of an established wage standard. On the other hand, the lack of a standard test for determining pay on the basis of efficiency results in many employees forming an utterly erroneous idea of their worth.

Now, this is a problem which can not be left altogether to employers to solve. It is the concern of every woman who works, if she is willing to do her share to improve conditions for every other woman who works. It is something for every business woman to think about. There are some possible solutions offered in the formation of unions for business women, where salary standards will be based on scientific tests for efficiency. The preparation of such tests is now being begun by a group of eminent psychologists cooperating with business men[1]. The results may pave the way for standardized and trustworthy salary scales. In the meantime, the woman who desires to know what is a just remuneration for her services can determine this for herself by a study of salary systems prevailing in many types of business. The methods of compensation prevalent to-day are: (1) Salary or wage payment, weekly or monthly; (2) Salary and bonus; (3) Salary and commission; (4) Piece-rate, or commission; (5) Profit-sharing, in addition to salary and other payments.

Office workers are usually paid on a straight salary basis, altho there are a few organizations where an additional bonus is paid in order to take care of the higher efficiency of some employees over others. For example, a publishing company pays typewriter operators in some departments according to the amount of work they produce; a girl who can write 100 square inches an hour being paid $10 per week;

[1] Economic Psychology Association, New York.

others are paid higher or lower on a similar scale. Other concerns use the cyclometer to count the per letter production and their salary scale is adjusted to the amount of production.

The bonus system can not be applied in all cases because of the varying conditions which affect the work of operators. For example, a stenographer who is highly capable may work for a dictator who is very slow, but whose correspondence is important. Her compensation, therefore, could not be fixt according to the quantity of the letters she wrote. She might have her work judged by the accuracy and intelligence shown, and possibly a bonus might be paid her in inverse ratio to the number of errors, altho it would be a complicated matter to keep accurate check on this factor.

In other branches of office work, this bonus (or piece-work plan) has been applied with good results. For example, in the accounting departments where there is an even flow of work an employee may develop as much speed as she is capable of, without being dependent on some one else to give her work enough rapidly. This is true also in the circularizing, order and other clerical departments.

The "bonus" is not necessarily a part of the weekly wage plan; nor is it always in the shape of money. The "prize contest" which is operated for a brief period of a few weeks or months is sometimes used to stimulate the organization as a whole, and also to discover the relative efficiency of various employees. For example, one mail-order house announced that at the end of three months $500 would be divided among the ten members of the correspondence department, in sums varying according to the amount of business produced. As each correspondent covered only three or four states, he received credit for all orders which came from that territory. At the end of three months, the man from whose territory the most orders had been received, received the highest bonus, $100; the next in order, $80, and so on.

The inequalities in the territories themselves affected the total sales as much as (and probably more than) the individual efficiency of the correspondents. But by comparing the results of the contest with the sales of previous years in that territory, it was possible to form a fairly dependable judgment of the relative ability of various correspondents, regardless of their standing in the contest.

Prize contests are more stimulative as a method of paying a bonus than some other methods in which it is inevitable that the results will be affected by conditions other than personal ability. Employees usually respond with interest to the idea of a prize contest. When a contest fails it is generally because of slipshod or inadequate management. It is rarely possible to offer a fixt sum for maximum production. There are generally factors beyond the employee's control which affect the sum total of results, and the bonus, or prize, system which succeeds is flexible enough to allow for exceptional conditions.

Then there is the "Point System," by which a record is kept of the current efficiency of each employee. At the end of six months or a year this is used as a basis on which to determine salary. For perfect attendance during the six months (barring absence or tardiness for excused reasons)

20 points are given. Perhaps five points are deducted for each lateness or absence. Sixty points might be allowed for perfect work, and deductions made for errors; 20 points for special service rendered outside of the immediate duties of the post. This is used by some (in varying forms) as a basis on which to award a bonus, or advancement in responsibility.

Another species of "bonus" is the practise of paying for accepted suggestions for bettering service. It is a common custom for most large organizations to have a "suggestion box" where employees deposit slips containing their suggestions for improvement. Accepted ideas are paid for at the rate of 50 cents or $1 apiece, or more. It happens, however, that interest in the "suggestion box" dwindles after it has been in operation for a time. Then an additional stimulus that may be applied is the announcement that accepted ideas will be paid for, not at the standard price of $1 or $2 apiece, but in accordance with the saving which they affect. A really good idea may save thousands of dollars, or add greatly to the good will, which can not be fixt at so many dollars' value but which is highly important nevertheless. If the employee is assured that she will receive a generous share in the profits of her suggestions, she is more than ever on the alert to please and to watch for possible improvements.

One advertising agency has a "merit committee" which meets regularly to decide what shall be paid certain employees for meritorious service rendered above their actual duty. For example, an employee who discovered an error in an advertising schedule was paid $10. Another who, on his own initiative, stayed after closing hours to push through an important shipment, was awarded $5. In addition, the names of employees making good suggestions were posted on a bulletin board in the office as stimulus to further effort.

Commission, either with or without salaries, is a form of payment usually made only to producers of business, salespeople doing inside or outside work. This is sometimes supplemented by a salary, or a "drawing account." For example, one typewriter company has for years hired all its salesmen on a standard basis of $10 a week salary and 10 per cent. commission. Exceptionally high-class salesmen in many other fields work on the strict commission basis. Indeed, only an expert salesman can afford to work permanently on this plan. A "drawing account" may be given him, and this is simply a weekly advance charged against commissions, so that he has funds regularly, even when there is a sudden lapse of business and he can obtain no orders.

While profit-sharing may seem an ideally just method of remuneration, as yet comparatively few plans have given entire satisfaction both to employers and employees. It is claimed that employees grow disgruntled and indifferent to their work when a lean year comes and there are no profits to share, feeling that they have been cheated out of an expected compensation. Sometimes, when stock is given instead of cash, an employee has to sacrifice his stock when he leaves the company, an anticipation which makes his holdings seem borrowed and not actual earnings.

Profit-sharing can not be regarded as the magic panacea to overcome compensation difficulties, but there are several plans of profit-sharing that have been satisfactory to all concerned. If employees are paid reasonable salaries, even a small share in the year's profits produces much good will, because it seems real profit-sharing. This is in contrast to some concerns where the "profit-sharing" plan is used as a bait to tempt employees to work for exceptionally low salaries, and the profits distributed do not bring their salaries beyond a low average. Sometimes a really good profit-sharing plan is spoiled by having the profits distributed in a paternal spirit. Profit-sharing is not welfare work. In the best type of organizations employees are made to feel that they have actually produced the profit by extra efforts in increasing production, preventing waste, etc. This leads to not only a more contented spirit, but conveys to employees a sense of responsibility which impels continued effort.

Indeed the success of profit-sharing plans has been shown to depend, not so much on the amount of profits shared, as on the justice with which it is distributed, and the spirit which is aroused. Merely to give a generous slice of profits may develop a grasping spirit, but where each employee is made to feel his responsibility, where he is encouraged to believe that he has a definite share in the business, there is more incentive to effort, greater cooperation, and more good will toward the house.

Pensions, sick benefits, and life insurance are other compensations paid by the modern employer, sometimes because of legislation and otherwise because of private policy. There are many excellent plans in operation, a typically good one affecting women as well as men being that of the American Telegraph and Telephone Co. All employees, men or women, who have served the company for 30 years or more may be retired and pensioned at the discretion of the company. Men 60 years of age or over, and women 55 years of age or over, who have served the company 20 years or more may retire; and any man of 55 or woman of 50 who has been with the company for 25 years or more may be retired at the discretion of the company. The pension paid is 1 per cent. of the average annual pay for each of the ten years of service preceding retirement, with a minimum of $20 per month.

For disability due to accidental injury while on the company's business, full salary or wages is paid for 13 weeks and half pay until the employee is able to earn a livelihood, or for the remainder of the disability, not exceeding six years in either case. For disability due to sickness or an accidental injury during employment but not in the performance of work for the company, benefits are paid in proportion to the years spent in the company's employ: Full pay for 13 weeks; half pay for 39 weeks if the term of employment is 10 years or more; full pay for 13 weeks and half pay for 13 weeks if the term of employment is five to 10 years; full pay for 4 weeks and half pay for nine weeks if the term of employment is two to five years.

If an employee meets death by accident due to performance of work by the company his or her dependent relatives are paid three years' wages, but not in excess of a total of $5,000. Employees in service five years, and having dependent relatives are insured in the sum of six months' wages; and those in service 10 years or more, in the sum of one year's wages, with a maximum of

$2,000. The sum is paid to the surviving relatives in the event of the employee's death.

It is best to have an understanding at the beginning of employment just what an employer pays and does not pay for, as this will prevent later friction and discontent. The customs of business firms vary as regards payments for work after hours, payments for absences, holidays, vacations, etc. It is best to know as soon as possible what these customs are. Of late years the tendency in business has been to eliminate the custom of working after hours. Years ago the exemplary clerk was the one who burned the midnight oil, but in a well-managed organization to-day, only the inefficient workers stay at night. As one executive put it: "When I was a young man, eager to get on, I worked over my books until 10 or 11 every night, and when the boss found it out he raised me 50 cents. But in the discretion of later years I realized that, if I had quit work at 6 o'clock and taken some recreation, I would have been fresh for my books at 8 o'clock next morning and could have done better work; hence I would not have had to stay at night. For this reason, if I find any one in my employ making a practise of staying at night in order to work, I fire him on the spot. Regular night work is an admission that the job is too much for the employee to handle during business hours. When a man admits that, he had better resign."

Conscientious office women are the strongest devotees to the night-work habit. There is no business habit more injurious and wasteful. If work is unusually heavy, one extra hour in the morning will be better than two at night. It is always possible to do quicker, better work in the morning than at the end of the day when drooping energies must be whipt and work is done on sheer nerve force.

In some organizations night-work at the beginning of each month, or some other special seasons like inventory-time, is considered necessary. The method of payment for such extra work considered most just is to pay so much per hour, generally a slightly higher sum in proportion than the salary scale of the worker. On the other hand, there are still some archaic business houses who pay their employees "50 cents for supper" and consider that as remuneration for three or four hours of extra work at night.

When a determined effort is made, it has been found entirely possible to eliminate night work entirely, either by anticipating the rush days and clearing desks for action in advance; or by arriving for an hour earlier than the schedule in the morning. Indeed, the experiment of shifting hours forward entirely has been made by a few organizations with good results. A few western firms opened their offices at seven in the morning, closing at 3:30 in the afternoon, during the summer months. The earlier rising in the morning harmed nobody, and the fact that employees were free in the afternoon for other interests and recreations was of immense benefit to them physically and mentally, and to the work of the next day.

The question of compensation for absences should also be understood in the beginning days of one's employment, because customs vary. Conscientious employees have occasionally suffered a lapse of loyalty when they discovered that they were charged for two days of sickness that kept them from their desks. This might occur in an organization that was eminently just in its dealings with employees, where night work was not demanded and every minute spent at work was paid for. Indeed, the system of payment for every hour spent at work according to the salary scale (including payment for legal holidays) and deductions for all absences, is considered by many the most dignified disposition of the problem.

Other firms make distinctions between voluntary and unavoidable absences. Salary continues to be paid if the employee claims absence is due to sickness, but this plan has its abuses. A typical example is a concern which found that there was a fixt percentage of daily absences because of the liberal stand of the company on this question. There was the usual representation of conscientious employees who would never remain away from their desks except for death. And these workers shouldered part of the burden of the unscrupulous women who habitually took a few days' leave of absence for every reasonable, and a few unreasonable, excuses. Shopping trips, excursions, the entertainment of visiting friends from other cities, illness of some member of the family unto the seventh remove—these proved to be the true causes of absence. But as soon as the company charged employees for days absent, there was a prompt and amazing drop in absences to a negligible percentage.

The solution worked out by one group of firms and which eventually proved most equitable to both employees and employers, was to allow each employee three days of absence per year at the company's expense, and no questions asked. Of course, it was understood that employees were not encouraged to take these days off, but they were permitted to do so, and no one asked whether it was for sickness, or shopping, or recreation. The employees' contribution to this scheme was that each had to learn to do some one else's work beside her own. In other words, the employees of each department were "interchangeable," so that the work would not suffer during any one's absence. Every employee understood that when she absented herself some other employee in her department was doing double duty. She could not console herself with the reflection that nobody lost by her absence because she would "make up for lost time to-morrow." Incidentally, the employee who was inclined to take advantage of the privilege and stayed away, often found speedy objection from other employees. Even if she justified frequent absences (after having used the three days per year allotted) by expressing her willingness to do so at her own expense, other employees who had to shoulder her duties brought pressure to bear, even before her remissness required disciplining from a higher authority.

It must be remembered, too, that business firms give their employees from six to nine holidays per year, and also from one or two weeks of vacation and sometimes more. In offices, a general custom is to allow two weeks' vacation with pay to all employees who have been with the company for one year. Some firms allow only one week to employees who have served them from six months to one year; two weeks to employees who have served two years and over. Sometimes even a longer vacation period is granted. It is only in backward, penurious firms that some vacation period is not provided. But as the typical modern employer pays for actual time spent at work, plus legal holidays and vacations, he should not be expected to pay for avoidable absences not due to company business.

V

ASKING FOR A RAISE; MAN'S REMUNERATION AND WOMAN'S

Eugene Field operated what was probably the most unique method of asking for a raise, and it was quite effective in its day. He addrest piteous, serio-comic appeals for more money to the cashier on the Chicago newspaper for which he wrote. If this failed, he absented himself from the office for three days. On the fourth day he sadly entered the business office, accompanied by a mournful petition for an increase in pay, and several of his young children clad in the rags of direst poverty.

Few business women have that exceeding gift of humor or the stage properties which enabled the genial Field to succeed in his schemes for screwing increases out of a close-fisted management. Perhaps even Field couldn't work his plan in a modern office, because there is nothing funny about asking for, or giving a raise. It isn't effective to use even the sentimental reason of faithful, long-time service. At best, that reason brings only small, sentimental increases in pay—and often not that.

Nevertheless, many employees cling to the idea that they should be advanced in salary regularly because of increased length of service. "I received an increase in pay at the end of the first year; why didn't I get more money this year?" wrote a young woman to the head of her department. Back came the honest reply: "You did better work at the end of the first year than at the beginning and you deserved more pay, but you have made no progress in the past year. You are not worth any more to us to-day than you were twelve months ago."

Now, it might seem that the girl who does the same work for two years improves automatically, but experience has shown that mere repetition of some task does not develop superior efficiency after a certain point is reached. For example, in one concern women were employed to compile lists from various sources. It took a girl several months to reach the common standard when she could produce a list of average length with only the average percentage of mistakes. Only a very exceptional girl exceeded the record. But at the end of two years of this work, the girl of average proficiency produced no greater amount of work than her average was at the end of the first year, with approximately the same minimum of errors.

In other words, there are types of work—generally the somewhat mechanical tasks—where average proficiency means reaching a certain "dead level" and subsequent experience does not develop superior skill. There is usually a salary limit for this dead level, and it is frequently the discouragement point for workers. Moreover, the stimulus of a possible higher reward being absent, the experienced worker is likely to be even more careless than the novice who works in anticipation of some advancement. In such a position, a girl can not insist on a raise. She has the alternative of getting out of the work into the next higher grade of occupation; or, if she is ingenious, she can try to evolve some plan for improving the work, saving steps, economizing time, work or expense in some way. Her evidence of ability to think will influence promotion.

Some firms, for example, the Metropolitan Life Insurance Company, or the Western Electric Company, divide all their office jobs into groups, with a minimum and maximum salary for each group. When an employee reaches the limit of salary and responsibility in one group, she knows she is in line for promotion to the next higher group where she will begin at the minimum, and gradually work up to the maximum salary, then rise to the next higher group, and so on. There are a few organizations where promotions in responsibility and salary are scientifically graded in this fashion. The tremendous advantage of such a system is that the purposeful employee sees her road clearly ahead, for a long distance. She can anticipate and prepare herself for responsibilities that are a long way off. She has also the constant stimulation of a definite reward for definite efforts.

Some business firms adhere to the custom of giving increases in pay only at certain periods of the year, such as January 1st, and at no other time, unless an employee succeeds to a more responsible post because of a sudden vacancy. While this plan has some advantage in that it provides a definite, regular time at least once a year for weighing each employee's efficiency and rewarding her accordingly, nevertheless a rigid ruling of this sort is likely to dampen the interest of the employee who finds on January 2nd that she is not in the chosen class and must wait another year for advancement. But if this is a strict ruling, the employee can make the most of it. Some months prior to the eventful season she places herself under serious self-examination, and makes a determined effort to improve her services, so that there will be no question about her promotion.

If there is no stated period for awarding increases, and the business woman feels that the time has come when she is justified in asking for more pay, she should do it in business-like fashion. First, she should be prepared with unanswerable proofs of advancement in work. If she can show that she has produced so much more business than she did six months ago, or has written so many more letters, or has made so many less errors and hence has improved her work such and such a percentage, or has saved money for the firm, or has submitted so many ideas for increasing business or saving, she has fine ammunition for winning.

On the other hand, the sentimental reason of long service, or of demanding of more pay because "If Miss Smith is paid that much I ought to have it too," rarely succeeds. There is generally some reason why Miss Smith is paid more, and it is best to know that reason before inviting a comparison.

Preferably an application for increase of pay should not be made verbally, but in writing. A personal request is likely to lead to argument, and good points may be forgotten during an animated discussion. The written application can be re-written twice or thrice, and revised until it embraces all the reasons, and is presented in strong, convincing language. If the written application does not sound convincing to the applicant, it will not convince the executive who receives it. It should, therefore, not be sent until there is a better and stronger basis for demanding an increase in pay.

If you can mentally assume the employer's position before asking for a raise, you may be able to write from his view-point, and with conviction. Consider yourself an employer. Last year you paid your seamstress $2 a day. Are you willing to pay her $3 a day now just because she has worked for you for some time? But, if she is now able to do twice as much work in one week as formerly, or if she does higher grade work, will you not consider it both just and profitable to engage her at the higher rate? So too, if you can cite proof of increased value in your application for an increase, if you can make your letter ring true and carry conviction, you will probably get your raise.

Many business women err, not so much in asking for a raise without cause, but in failing to ask for it when it is deserved. They are timid, but believe their value should be recognized by an increase in pay without the necessity of asking for it. Or they are so sensitive that they believe their dignity requires that they resign in case their request is refused. These are wholly fallacious notions. A business man of intelligence thinks none the less of an employee who sticks to her job at the same salary when he has given her a reason for refusing to pay her more. On the contrary, he is likely to respect her good sense in not hot-temperedly throwing away a position because of a few dollars. If you believe you are deserving of more, and a reasonable cause for refusal is not given you, then make sure you are right about your ability to fill a better paying job before you proudly send in your resignation.

Every woman is justified in insisting strenuously on good pay for good work. When all business women, as a class, will pursue this policy we will hear less frequently the complaint that a man doing the same work as a woman is receiving higher pay. Women do the cause of all women in business a grave injustice by accepting without protest lower pay than men for the same work. But we must distinguish between the woman who thinks she is doing a man's work, and the woman who actually is doing it.

One example is that of a public service corporation which dismissed a large number of office men, hired women in their places and paid the women considerably less than the men, but publicly boasted that the women were doing much better work. It was an absolute commercial sin for these women to accept the jobs solely and wholly on a basis of cheapness, because they could have received the same remuneration as the men had they stedfastly held out for it. The company admitted the women did better work, and saved money because it was necessary to employ fewer women than men to do the same amount of work. To have paid the women a salary equal to that paid each man, would have been only to divide the saving between employer and employee—a kind of profit-sharing system which is growing in favor even among soulless corporations. This is simply an illustration indicating how lack of organization and recognized salary standards in office work for women result in making poor jobs out of good jobs.

On the other hand, it is absurd for women in some positions to agitate or expect to receive pay equal to that of men. There are many women who are able private secretaries, or assistants to big men, but who cherish the idea that they are really doing the hardest part of the big man's job, and if justice were done, they would receive almost the same pay. It is a tribute to the executive ability of a man that he can unload the details of his job, so that his mind is left free to grapple with big problems. It is equally characteristic of such women that they consider the innumerable details which they handle so ably as constituting the whole of the big job.

Analysis of many such women assistants has shown that, while they are exceedingly efficient under the direction of a chief, there are few, very few, who would make equally able executives. They have not the daring, the initiative, the dynamic self-propulsion, the habit of swift, energetic action immediately on arriving at a decision that are part of the successful executive's equipment. The very fact that they are able secretaries and are expert in detail capacity, may be proof positive that they have not the large-plan executive type of mind. The biggest positions and pay are given to those with initiative and a willingness to assume heavy responsibilities. Large profits in business are the result of large plans and successful risk more than of plodding, faithful attention to details.

In the smaller positions, women do not and will not receive equal pay for equal work as men until they insist upon it as strongly as men do, until they are just as independent as men in refusing a "cheap" job which is below their standard, and until there is some means of influencing women to recognize and adhere to definite salary standards. In the larger jobs, women can equal men's successes when they possess the executive frame of mind. That involves a change of temperament and habits of mind from detail-faithfulness to large-plan foresight. What women are doing as executives and what they can do is outlined in a later chapter.

VI

EDUCATION IN BUSINESS, STIMULATION AND "WELFARE" WORK

A LARGE store found, upon investigation, that 60 per cent. of the girls employed had not completed the grammar grades in school; many of them did not even know fractions. Under the old hire-and-fire system, these inefficients would have been dismissed, but business has learned in recent years that the hire-and-fire system is tremendously wasteful, not only to the inadequate employee, but also to the business. It costs money to hire an employee. It costs money to give her whatever assistance she needs to launch her in her new work. In one firm, it was estimated that it costs about $30 to hire a man, check up his references, and get him started at work. Another business firm found that hiring a man, "breaking him in," then firing him and having to hire another to replace him, cost from $300 up. Some business firms try to avoid this waste by installing more scientific employment systems, so that the unfit will be rejected and there will be no costly experiments with inefficients. As long as men and women were thrust into business with inadequate education, there would be an army of workers who, even tho potentially able, were temporarily in the class of the unfit.

The more constructive method has been found to be the education of workers, so that they can handle better their particular tasks. Business has taken the matter of educating employees into its own hands, and to-day the "corporation school" is found in large factories and shops, stores and offices. Several methods of instruction are used:

(1) Actual class-rooms are installed in the plant of the corporation, where special instructors teach elementary subjects, or subjects relating directly to the business.

(2) The local educational system may provide instructors in elementary subjects to teach employees; the local educational system bears the expense of the instructor, but the business pays the worker for time spent at "school."

(3) The "continuation school." Under this plan school students spent part of their time in a business organization, and part in school or high school. This is, in effect, a direct co-operation between the school and business, and theoretical training and actual practise are thus combined.

Wisconsin now provides for a "continuation school" in every city in the state that has a population over 5,000. Children between 14 and 16 years of age who are at work are required to attend. Following is a description of the actual workings of a typical "corporation school" operated by a mail-order house, an especially large school, but it is selected to indicate the wide scope of information that may be required of office workers—information which business demands and which the average schooling does not afford. This school has a purpose similar to most corporation schools, *i.e.*, to provide training which shall make up for deficiencies in elemental education; to enable employees doing uncongenial work to know other branches of the business, so that they may select work for which they think they are better fitted; to instruct employees in correct business practise, and to stimulate them to a larger view-point about the business as a whole, so as to encourage the ambitious.

The teaching staff of the school consists of women who are trained teachers. They prepare material for lessons, and this is standardized and kept in a loose-leaf manual for permanent reference. This manual gives details of the practise of every department the workings of which are taught in the school. Instruction proceeds gradually from the theoretical to the practical, so that, by the time a student has completed a course, she has been doing the actual work of a department, and may at once fill a position.

Employees receive instruction for about one hour daily during business hours. The length of their course varies according to their needs, from one week to three months, but they are paid for time spent at the company's school. As a rule, there are about 20 persons in a class, and the daily attendance at the school varies from 450 to 750, keeping very busy a staff of 12 teachers and one principal. A systematic record is kept of every pupil-employee, both as to school grading and rating in work later. These records are used to determine the value of the employee, deciding promotions, etc.

OUTLINE OF CLASSES AND STUDIES IN A CORPORATION SCHOOL

General Classes

Arithmetic
Composition
Geography
Grammar
Hygiene
Penmanship
Rapid Calculation
Spanish
Spelling
Typing

General Office Classes

Adjusting for Division heads and assistants
Adjusting for head adjusters
Combination adjusting
Complaints
Correspondence
Filing
Head clerk's work
Head Order clerk's work
Mail examining
Mail reading
Order advising
Order examining
Order writing
Returned goods adjusting
Teller work

Departmental Classes

Assembly Department	Assembly sheets
Back order Department	B/O writing, filing answering inquiries
Cashier's Department	
Credit and Refund	
Duplicating	Duplicating, routing, zoning, order examining
Efficiency	
Mail entry	
Merchandise	Merchandise sheets
Merchandise examining	Listing, tagging, examining
Returned goods Department	Package opening, merchandise examining
Sales checking Department	Ledger work, sales checking, order advising
Sheet analyzing	
Shipping	C.O.D. shipments, adjusting, label writing
Stencil	
Traffic	Proofreading and filing

In addition, there are illustrated lectures on the activities of various departments which are given frequently during the year. All employees attend at least one lecture. Often the lectures are followed by a trip through the department when operations are explained by the teacher in charge.

Here we have the typically "office" school.

But there are two other types of schools which in business are operated in order to develop employees. One is the technical school, in which employees are taught manufacturing or technical subjects peculiar to the business. Some of the best technical schools are operated by railroad companies, public service companies, manufacturers of tools, machinery, etc. For example, the New York Edison Company has one of the finest technical schools for employees in the country. Here are given courses in the elements of physics, electrical engineering, thermodynamics, etc., which increase the potentialities of employees, but which few workers get owing to the long courses prescribed in good outside training-schools.

The third type of corporation school is the "sales school." This may be subdivided into schools which teach wholesale selling and schools which teach retail selling. Perhaps there is no other branch of work in which there existed a greater need for educating employees than in the retail selling field. The "department store salesgirl" is the perennial example of inefficiency and indifference, because the public comes more in contact with her than with any other class of woman worker. It is not that her deficiencies are greater, but that they are more obvious. She suffers from lack of preparation, and hence many department stores have installed schools for training women in the technique of selling. In Boston there is the famous Union School of Salesmanship for Women, which was begun as an independent enterprise by Mrs. Lucinda W. Prince, but which is now cooperating closely with local department stores. There is an advisory committee made up of executives from each of the cooperating stores. The students are all saleswomen employed in these stores. They divide the day between the school and the store. The girls ring in their time in the school just as they do in the store; they receive full pay for school time, and are disciplined by the store for school lateness or for absence. Whether or not this scheme pays can be judged by the statement of one store official who declared that the girls who attend the course sell more goods in the afternoon in the store than the girls without instruction sold the entire day. Selling science, store system, knowledge of stock, personal hygiene, are the subjects taught The following questions from examination papers indicate the scope of instruction given:

> Give all the tests for a good piece of cotton sheeting, dress linen, broadcloth, taffeta.
>
> Describe the "weighting" process in silk.
>
> Suggest three ways of finding out the price a customer is willing to pay.
>
> Give five talking points on an article you are now selling.
>
> If you have a customer who has always worn out-of-fashion styles, how can you sell her an up-to-date model with which she will feel satisfied when she has it at home?

In New York the Department Store Educational Association is performing somewhat similar service by providing standardized instruction to saleswomen at the expense, and on the premises, of cooperating department stores. The women are exceedingly responsive. The great benefit of the plan lies in this point: not only does the school educate the saleswoman, but, by arousing her interest in the history of the articles she sells she is filled with a new zest for her job. She grows to care for her work for its own sake, and develops an appetite for business information which keeps her happy and ambitious for progress.

Most of the large organizations that employ many "road salesmen" have found it most practical to train a man in their own school before permitting him to go out to sell goods. The field for outside saleswomen is as yet limited, but there are a few concerns employing traveling saleswomen (for example, a prominent corset company). In a few instances these women, too, receive training in school before they attempt to get business. The "school" for outside salespeople may either be actual classroom work at the plant of the company, or it may be a correspondence course, or it may be weekly or monthly lectures at the branch offices. Sometimes this educational work is supplemented by frequent conventions which are, in effect, schools, because regular lectures are given, plus the additional benefit conferred on the younger salesmen of having the opportunity to listen to the wisdom of veterans on the road. Further details of stimulation and educational plans for outside salesmen are given in Chapter XV.

Educational and stimulation methods for employees dovetail somewhat, and may be summarized as follows:

(1) Actual school work, with equipped classrooms and permanent instructors. Unquestionably this is the most thorough. But it is also costly, and so some of the smaller organizations where expenses must be kept down have substituted other plans among the following educational methods:

(2) Weekly lectures on various branches of work. These lectures are delivered, either by outside specialists like office systematizers, efficiency engineers, sales experts, special instructors from colleges or business lecturers, alternating with executives of company and department heads.

(3) Maintaining a business library for employees. Here are kept carefully selected books relating to the industry, trade journals, clippings from newspapers and magazines, and good books on the principles of business.

(4) House meetings. This may be called a system of self-education. Weekly or bi-weekly the employees to meet to discuss experiences, ideas for business development, and problems of work. The most successful types of meetings are those presided over by an employee, not by an

executive, so that meetings are free from restraint. All suggestions and complaints are given impartial consideration, and the greatest frankness is encouraged. Consequently, the covert criticism or disgruntled spirit arising from concealed discontent is eliminated.

(5) Building an "instruction manual." This is developed from suggestions and rulings at the house meetings and is supplemented by information from executives and by expert outside counsel. The manual usually contains very clear explanations of every detail of work; hours, specific duties of each post, possible emergency duties, details of routine or "standard practise" instruction; sources of supplementary information; errors to be avoided, all based on the experience of employees in the organization. Before an employee is entrusted with responsibility, she gives proof or attests over her signature that she has read the "Manual."

The "Manual" has been the means of drilling salesmen and other employees for some of the best-organized business institutions in the country. In some cases, salesmen have been required to memorize the manual completely, and actually to use the standard phrases of argument, "approach," "close" etc. As these arguments were prepared by experts, they were remarkably effective in the beginning, even when used by inexperienced salesmen. However, the plan was later abandoned when it was found that men committed stereotyped arguments to memory, without taking the trouble to digest the facts, and so acquired the habit of selling mechanically. A sudden and unexpected objection, therefore, would leave them utterly at a loss for a convincing reply. Now, many salesmen carry the "manual of objections" which has been developed by experienced men, and which is used for reference only when an unusual situation arises.

(6) House organs. These are publications issued periodically, and devoted to facts about the company or its employees. There are house organs edited for customers, too, but we are considering here the educational value of the house organ for employees. Usually it is edited by employees, altho it may contain authoritative articles on branches of the business by an executive. The house organ confines itself to helpful ideas, suggestions, criticisms, etc., affecting the individual business. Also, it devotes some space to "personals" about members of the organization.

(7) Suggestion-box. The idea-fulness of employees is one of the valuable byproducts of business.

Many business houses keep conspicuous a permanent "suggestion-box" to receive ideas. Sometimes the suggestions are typed on a plain white sheet, unsigned, but with the sender's name inside on an attached, sealed envelop. This is to insure fair consideration of the idea, as the examiners do not know until the idea is passed on whether it proceeds from the humblest clerk or the most important official. Enlightened organizations encourage exchange of suggestions between departments rather than the overzealous department spirit which views every other branch of the business as an enemy to be fought and outwitted. Sometimes prizes are given each month for the best accepted suggestions, ranging from $1 up; or perhaps the idea is paid for according to its value, the amount of time or money its adoption saves, or the improvement it affects. Careful record is kept of the writers of suggestions, to be used as a basis for judging promotions.

(8) Prize contests, while not strictly educational work in the pedagogic sense, provide, nevertheless, an excellent stimulus to the inert organization. Prize contests, properly managed, are to some extent a stimulus to self-education and awaken new spurts of effort.

The contest spirit is almost an elemental one.

It is one of the most effective means for stimulating sales, even at those periods of the year when a decrease is considered normal, and many organizations use prize contests regularly as a part of their sales-management methods. In one company the prize for high sales quotas is a sum of money, or commodities like an auto, or trips to a convention. Generally the commodity prize is found more stimulating than the prize of money. Somehow, it seems to stimulate the imagination more, or, as one salesman put it, "the money is spent and forgotten, but a prize is a permanent reminder of a victory."

One office appliance concern, whose sales usually dropt considerably in the summer months, succeeded in running sales up to a higher sum than normal months, produced by operating a "prize-less" sales contest. The sales manager of this concern was very popular with the men, and while he was on his vacation the advertising manager conceived the idea of starting a sales contest among the men as a testimonial to the sales manager. The plan worked beautifully. Even the older, more experienced men (who had hitherto cherished a secret opposition to prize contests, because they considered them undignified and an implication that they would not produce business unless egged on by the hope of a prize) redoubled efforts as an evidence of esteem for their chief. A life insurance company has made use of this same stimulus of "regard for the president" to arouse thousands of agents to greater enthusiasm.

The prize contest has been used in office work, too, with success. One advertiser doubled the output of the circularizing department simply by announcing that each girl's output, and the number of errors per day, would be written on a blackboard in the room. Immediately girls who had been addressing 400 folders per day jumped their efforts 50 per cent.; and when the management announced that there would be a 25 per cent. increase in pay to girls who reached a certain maximum, the really efficient workers attained that maximum, and the incompetents dropt out automatically. While this is often criticized as "driving," it must be recognized that it is equally unjust to have the salaries of a whole department down at a low point because lazy or inefficient members of the department keep the average down. The prize contest has been used in all departments of office work where results are measurable, and production and number of errors can be known.

(9) Conventions. This is a stimulation plan employed mainly by firms who have a large staff of salesmen. The modern type of convention is one of the finest methods of education and stimulation. The old-fashioned "convention" was generally more of an excuse for jollification than anything else. But it was found to be utterly wasteful and has been superseded by a better type. The convention to-day is managed on more methodical lines. The salesmen know some time before what the program is to be for each of the three or four days that they are assembled. A typical program includes:

(a) Addresses on salesmanship, by specialists, by the sales manager, and by some of the salesmen themselves.

(b) Demonstration sales. Two of the salesmen engage in a "mock sale" on the platform, to demonstrate how sales are made, objections met, etc. These "lessons" are hugely enjoyed by salesmen and are profitable to older as well as the new men.

(c) Addresses by department heads, to familiarize salesmen with the working of the entire business: advertising manager, factory manager, credit department, complaint and adjustments department, shipping; and some executives, the president or the general manager, may give talks on the policy of the company and the contemplated changes.

(d) A trip through factory to observe actual manufacturing processes.

There are some social functions in the evening or afternoons to get the men together on a more intimate basis. But the great value of these conventions lies in the informal "getting-together" of the men, the exchange of experience and mutual help.

These conventions provide an excellent opportunity for the management to "size up" different men and get a better basis for judging their character. One manufacturer, whose plant is in a small New England town, notified his salesmen that they have *carte blanche* to order anything they like when they are his guests. Local dealers are ordered to give the salesmen anything they desire, but a record is kept of everything each salesman orders. This gives the manufacturer an additional glimpse into the character of the men—which men take stimulants, which abuse the privilege, etc.

The value of the corporation school is unquestioned, but many plans had to be experimented with before an efficient type of school was developed. In order to preserve records of experience and to assist organizations in the operation of schools, the National Association of Corporation Schools was founded some years ago. Its members are commercial or governmental organizations interested in the education of employees, instructors, and other individuals in sympathy with the objects of the association.

Its objects are "to render new corporation schools successful from the start, by warning them against the pitfalls into which others have fallen and to provide a forum where corporation school officers may exchange experiences." Its functions are "to develop the efficiency of the individual employee; to increase efficiency in industry; and to have the courses in established educational institutions modified to meet more fully the needs of industry." The headquarters of the Association are at Irving Place and 15th Street, New York. The president is John McLeod of the Carnegie Steel Company, and the executive secretary,

F. C. Henderschott of the New York Edison Company. Reports are furnished to members, and a monthly bulletin is issued containing data about current activities in educational and vocational work.

"Educational work" and so-called "welfare work" for employees are sometimes confused, but there is a sharp distinction between the two. Educational work is some type of schooling. It is a frank endeavor on the part of corporations to make their employees more efficient, so that they may be more profitable to the company as well as to themselves. "Welfare work" on the other hand, is concerned more with the physical comfort and recreation for the worker, even tho its ultimate aim is the same, that is, to produce happier, and therefore more efficient workers. The following are the methods classified as Employers' Welfare Work:

(1) Rest-room for employees.
(2) Reading-rooms and library.
(3) Club-house or auditorium for entertainment.
(4) Hospital room in plant for emergency cases.

REST-ROOM FOR EMPLOYEES OF THE NATIONAL CLOAK & SUIT CO., NEW YORK

(5) Supplying luncheons at low price or cost.

(6) Savings bank in plant, where employees are encouraged to save regularly, and where they can obtain loans at reasonable interest.

(7) Appointing workmen inside the plant to make investigations regularly, and report recommendations to management for better equipment to safeguard health of workers.

(8) Providing "model" homes for employees at low rental.

(9) Establishment of classes for employees' families—in cooking, gardening, rudimentary branches of education; or engaging a trained dietician to visit workmen's families and teach their wives better cooking and housekeeping.

(10) Encouraging gardening and home beautifying among employees by offer of prizes.

Many of these plans, like building homes, or club-houses, or providing education for employees' families are necessary only in such large organizations as are removed from city facilities for adequate housing and entertainment. The rest-rooms, auditorium, etc., are regarded as highly valuable, especially in those plants where there is much monotonous labor. For example, in a food-packing concern, the girls have a fifteen-minute rest period in the morning and another in the afternoon when they go to the auditorium for playing and dancing. After this little bit of recreation, there is more desire to work with keenness and rapidity at a monotonous task, and there is less dreariness and "soldiering" at work than if every one was required to work at a monotonous job for four or five hours without a break. The rest period is as essential as the rest-room, which is valueless if the employees have no time to go there!

There are so many beneficial aspects to various types of "welfare" work that it is astonishing to find how often the work is an utter failure. We hear complaints that employees do not appreciate it, or do not even use the facilities provided. A New York department store installed a beautiful gymnasium—only to find that the saleswomen never ventured into it. Most of these employees were city-bred women about thirty years old, or more. The idea of jumping around in a gymnasium appeared to them undignified and unattractive. Finally, a tactful physical director met the situation by inaugurating a series of lessons in which she explained the relation between exercise and physical efficiency.

Many of the unions decry "welfare work," as only a sop to underpaid employees. Employees are generally quite ready to believe that they are not receiving all the compensation they deserve, and that the philanthropic rest-room and gymnasium come from sums diverted from their pay-envelop. Consequently they resent the paternalism that can afford to give with one hand because it withholds with the other. Nevertheless, it has been shown that strikes are fewer in concerns operating welfare plans than in similar plants minus this philanthropy. These corporations are generally noted for their eminently just treatment of employees in all respects.

This is the very heart of the situation. Welfare work succeeds when it is a supplementary friendly expression to employees who are well treated and adequately paid. Welfare work fails when it is used as a surface panacea to a fundamentally wrong industrial condition. Rest-rooms are of no value to the girl who has to work unreasonably long hours. Nor is the corporation lunch-room much of a help to the girl who earns so little that she can not afford three square meals a day, and suffers from chronic malnutrition. But the attitude of employers is becoming more and more enlightened. The time is not far distant when adequate lighting, sanitary washrooms, rest-rooms, hospital rooms, etc., will be looked upon as a necessary part of a company's standing equipment to facilitate production —and not as "employees' welfare work" which is to be regarded as philanthropy.

The greatest help to employees is education. Education teaches the employee how to work, and how to live. When she is a better producer for the company and for herself she can pay her share in any project for entertainment and advancement.

Some corporations operate a plan, whereby the management bears only part of the expense of school, or "welfare," work. Indeed, even some concerns which spend considerable money on educational methods for salesmen require that salesmen bear some part of the expense—perhaps it is for text-books, or for expenses traveling to the school. The effect is highly beneficial. Employees have a greater interest in a plan of schooling, or of advancement, in which they have invested some of their own money. There is also a feeling of independence and self-reliance which does more to develop strength and efficiency than the acceptance of corporation benevolence.[1]

[1] For details of many plans of Welfare Work, see Bulletin No. 123 on "Employers' Welfare Work," published by U. S. Dept. of Labor, Washington. Also Bulletins of the National Association of Corporation Schools.

VII

HABITS THAT HELP THE BUSINESS WOMAN

"When I have an important commission to give to some one on my staff, I generally prefer the individual with mediocre ability, but absolutely reliable habits, to the brilliant but erratic person of irresponsible habits," remarked a business executive who employs a large staff of women assistants. Examine the organization rules of successful firms, and you will find that the question of habits is one of enormous importance. The observable habits of employees influence promotions more than variations in efficiency. Here is a corporation employing hundreds of women clerks, that keeps careful record of their status on this basis: Accuracy, Appearance, Quantity of work produced, Industry and steady application, Observance of office rules, Care in handling company's property, Courtesy and good will toward fellow employees, Initiative and executive ability, Suggestions made, Number of times late, Number of days or hours absent.

Note that out of eleven of these qualities eight are simply personal habits. Whenever the weeding-out process is in operation, you will find that dismissals are based largely on objectionable habits, and that the judging of personal ability is influenced by knowledge of personal habits. What you are is the consequence of what you do—of what is your "round of daily behavior." Therefore, we can not escape the fact that the greatest aid to success is the conscious formation of good habits at the beginning of a career. Prof. William James states in his essay on "Habit" that "The period between twenty and thirty is the critical one in the formation of intellectual and professional habits; below twenty is the more important period still for the fixing of personal habits. In most of us, by the age of thirty, the character has set like plaster, and will never soften again."

Think of some one you know who possesses a conspicuous personal habit. Does not that habit affect his whole character, directly and indirectly? It is said of President Wilson that his two most conspicuous personal habits are extreme neatness and extreme punctuality. His shorthand notes for his own use are always so precise that they are legible to others. His own observance of and insistence on absolute punctuality are famous. A moment's tardiness is an unforgivable sin. All destructive habits like tardiness, carelessness, "scatteration" instead of concentration, handicap us because they are a perpetual source of irritation. Good habits, on the other hand, become part of us so that we act almost without conscious effort.

A business is like the human body. Within there is a highly complex system of nerves and muscles, but their agreeable coordination results in an outwardly calm, smoothly working unit. Each tiny nerve and cell has its own responsibility—none is too insignificant to neglect any part of its functioning. The discomfort from a cut finger, or a rebellious digestion, extends in some measure to the entire system. So, too, the laxness of one individual in a business is bound to injure in some degree the workings of the organization as a whole.

The office woman sometimes excuses her appearance at 9:30 instead of 9 o'clock on the ground that she "always makes up for it by one or two hours' extra work in the evening." This individual shifting of hours is not in the least beneficial. Morning lateness can not be counteracted by night work, because the delay of one worker in the morning delays the chain of work and hampers other employees.

The habit of tardiness has a personal reaction on character. The tardy individual is generally "easy-going," a good promiser, and an equally good eluder of responsibilities, for the easiest thing in the world to make, and break, is a lax person's promise. This type of business woman sometimes discovers with a shock that her casual acquiescence to a request is regarded as a solemn promise which she is expected to fulfil, regardless of the personal inconvenience it may cause her. The customer who asks that her order be delivered earlier than conveniently possible does not want to be placated by a promise; she expects fulfilment. When an executive asks mildly that a certain piece of work be done "when you have time," he accepts acquiescence as a promise to do the work some time soon, and not as an indefinite postponement. Promptness in fulfilling obligations is the basis of a reputation for reliability; neglect is an open door to a more earnest competitor to enter.

Initiative—that little tin god of business—is a habit pure and simple. The girl who develops the habit of shoving aside any problem or piece of information that does not affect her immediate job will stick to that particular job forever and a day. "I'm not paid to make out invoices," remarked a young stenographer when asked to help temporarily. She prides herself on the fact that she stuck to the work which she had been "hired to do." She then deliberately closed all doors to further information and promotion by her habit of sticking to her tiny groove.

On the other hand, there is a type of young woman who is the "star" in every office. She knows something about every branch of the business. She is an omnivorous reader of everything that relates to the business as a whole. She is forever asking questions. She is forever making suggestions, and the fact that nine out of ten are refused does not daunt her in the least. Initiative is an unconscious habit with her and she keeps on exercising it until she wins an executive post on the strength of it.

The great help to success in business is to adjust all habits persistently so that they fit into the twofold purpose of business which is (1) to render service; (2) to yield a profit. These two are related inseparably. The business man who endeavors to operate his business while both eyes are fastened on profit, so that only indifferent service is rendered customers, deliberately invites disaster. Similarly, a business that is not operated economically so as to yield a profit will not long continue to give service.

These facts apply equally to the individual worker. A single-minded devotion to the pay-envelop results in indifferent service; so giving good service for less than its worth is self-robbery, and cheapens the ultimate value of one's services.

Now, how do personal habits affect service rendered, or the profits of business? First, consider the relation of business to the public. Service depends on the habits of scrupulous honesty, reliability and courtesy on the part of the entire organization, executives and minor employees alike. Indifference or carelessness on the part of any member of the organization may mean defective goods, delayed delivery or offended customers. There is not any part of the relationship between business and customer that is small enough to be neglected.

Even the ostensibly trivial service of receiving callers is of greater importance than is believed by business men who are willing to be represented in the outer office by raw little boys. The character of an organization is judged from the first impression, and that first impression is often made in the reception room. The woman who receives or interviews callers has a fine responsibility. She needs the diplomacy of a Metternich, the manners of a Chesterfield, and the optimism of a Munyon, all combined in an agreeable personality, not ostentatiously attractive. Incidentally, in acquiring these qualities she will develop a poise and personal charm that will serve her well in outside interests. The brusque demand, "Your card, please," perhaps followed by a suspicious "Have you an appointment?" has ruffled the feelings of many a caller, so that it was doubly difficult for the man in the inner office to complete a business transaction with him. A neat personal appearance, a cheerful and dignified demeanor, and essential good manners are the requisites for the woman who receives business callers. Sometimes natural nervousness will make her put questions brusquely. In that case, it is best for her to study a regular formula of courteous greeting and inquiry, and in time the habit will relieve embarrassment and impart self-confidence.

Just as important as the polite reception of desirable visitors is the art of politely disposing of undesirable ones. There is in the business world a curious tribe of chronic visitors, men who doubtless have some affairs of their own, but in some miraculous way seem to have plenty of time to pay innumerable futile, time-wasting calls. Sometimes they are pestiferously persistent salesmen pursuing an impossible order; sometimes they are information seekers who do not know when it is time to go; and sometimes they are simply unquenchable conversationalists. Every office would benefit by keeping a card index of the chronic caller tribe, so that the diplomatic woman in the reception room knows they are not to be announced. Indeed, a reception clerk who could compile such a list and keep to it would more than pay her own salary in the time saved for important executives.

The appearance of the office also plays an important part in the impression produced on visiting customers or other callers. The desk piled heaven-high with papers is no longer considered a sign of prosperous "busy-ness" or conscientious industry. In the well-managed office it is an evidence of personal inefficiency to have on the desk anything except the subject worked on at the time. For this reason, the modern office no longer installs the cumbersome, roll-top desk with innumerable pigeonholes, which are just minature graveyards for burying the work we don't want to do! The ideal working-desk is the flat-top desk with two or three drawers. These drawers contain only stationery and writing material. There is never any correspondence inside any one's desk; and no one may keep correspondence for more than twenty-four hours. Near the end of the day the undisposed-of matter goes into the files, to be called out the following morning. But no correspondence can be "lost" for an indefinite period, only to be unearthed later in the mound of papers on somebody's desk. In addition, it is a spur to activity to have before you only the work you can do now, and get it out of the way so that the desk is cleared frequently for new tasks.

In the business woman's relations with her co-workers, the habit of priceless value is tact—the fine art of avoiding offense, or inconvenience to others. When she must criticize, she will be a courteous, constructive critic. There is a pessimistic atmosphere in the office which harbors the disparaging, perpetual critic, ever on the alert to declare "That's wrong," "You can't do it," etc. Criticism is a necessity, and constructive criticism from a logical individual is a liberal education. It has been said of Elihu Root that he is the rare lawyer who would tell you what you could do when other lights of the law were able to tell only what you could not do.

A full knowledge of all the facts is a requisite for intelligent criticism, and the only worth-while criticism is constructive suggestion. If you can not indicate a better way, let the criticism go unspoken, for it is possible that the worker selected the best means out of many unsatisfactory possibilities, even tho that best fell short of perfection. One business man made it a rule never to listen to a criticism unaccompanied by a constructive suggestion. "Any one can tell me where I'm wrong; what I want to know is a way to make it right."

Interruptions are often a necessary annoyance requiring tactful handling. Of course, it is better to interrupt an authority with a question than to proceed ignorantly with the possibility of wastefully repeating ancient errors. But when you must interrupt, interrupt on paper. Verbal questions begin conversations, digressions, and waste time invariably, while the written message brings a brief, direct answer. Unhappy is the lot of the girl who achieves an office reputation as a mathematician, etymologist or expert speller. Questions are hurled at her unceasingly, and while this may, for a time, flatter her, eventually the loss of time she sustains, and the break in her concentration, count against her work.

A handbook of English, a dictionary, perhaps also a trade reference book, are the most useful ornaments on the desk of every woman who has to write or dictate a letter! Don't interrupt the office authority if there is any possibility that the information you seek is in files or reference books. But, if you can't possibly find the information, better confess ignorance than errors.

To prevent errors, many efficient organizations to-day keep a written "'manual" containing records of standard practise in daily work for every job in the company; also suggestions and corrections, so that when a new employee reads the manual she is adequately informed from a trustworthy source. She is not quite as likely to make errors as when she is expected to pick up whatever she can from another clerk or her daily routine. This "manual" represents practically the accumulated experience of workers, the most important asset in preventing waste. It is prepared in several ways; sometimes as a result of "house meetings," where employees' problems are discust among themselves; or by motion studies of each individual's work, and by making "standard practise" instructions for each kind of work. Employees cooperate by writing experiences, giving new ideas for improvement, and so helping to build a complete and reliable manual.

The second function of business, yielding a profit, is dependent not only on large sales, but on the economical administration of the business. Some one once interpreted a thrifty Frenchwoman's opinion of an American housewife into this: "She spills into the garbage pail more than her husband can shovel into the front door." A thousand and one infinitesimally small business leaks can melt a huge potential profit into nothingness. Consequently, every employee is responsible for some measure of economy. It is just as much her job to conserve supplies as to do good work. Indeed, in some of the non-creative positions, the only opportunity for advancement lies in the ability of the worker to save time and cut costs. Specialists are often hired to find "small leaks." But the business woman with the economy habit can discover them herself, save her firm money, and incidentally achieve personal glory convertible into personal profit!

How can one think of possible business economies? There are two divisions of economy: (1) Economy in right buying; (2) Economy in avoiding waste.

You can help by developing your knowledge of business tools. What are the newest and best labor-savers? Is this a costly machine that will be used rarely, or will it be used enough to realize a profit on the investment? What can be done with the time saved through the use of this machine? Have you available the catalogs of all manufacturers of the supplies you use? Do you know the difference in quality and cost between competitive articles?

In the second group are the innumerable small wastes—paper, envelops, carbon ribbons, etc. Why not dispense with the two-color ribbon, on the typewriter, if the red is used only rarely? Whenever red lettering is needed, simply insert a sheet of red carbon over the page. This will prevent the waste of throwing away a two-color ribbon, the black half of which is outworn, while the red half is practically new. In many offices yellow sheets for carbon letters are not used, the carbon copy being made on the back of the letter answered. Where hundreds of letters are written daily, the cost in paper and file space saved is considerable.

There are many other small leaks which the careful business woman can perceive. In addition, the habit of economy in business continues to personal economy. The woman who wastes not her employer's property wastes not her own. She who buys intelligently for her business develops the habit of shopping wisely for herself.

But, supposing all these desirable habits are not part of character, what then? Let me quote again from Professor James's article on "Habit": "The greatest thing, in all education, is to make our nervous system our ally instead of our enemy. We must make automatic as many useful actions as we can, and guard against growing into ways that are likely to be disadvantageous to us. In the acquisition of a new habit, we must (1) Take care to launch ourselves with as strong and decided an initiative as possible; (2) Never suffer an exception to occur until the new habit is securely rooted in your life. Each lapse is like the letting fall of a ball of string which one is carefully winding up; a single slip undoes more than a great many turns will wind again; (3) Seize the very first possible opportunity to act on every resolution you make.

"Finally, keep the faculty of effort alive by a little gratuitous exercise every day. That is, be systematically ascetic or heroic in little unnecessary points. Do every day or two something for no other reason than that you would rather not do it, so that when the hour of dire need draws nigh it may find you not unnerved and untrained to stand the test. Asceticism of this sort is like the insurance which a man pays on his house and goods. The tax does him no good at the time, and possibly may never bring him a return. But if the fire does come, his having paid it will be his salvation from ruin."

VIII

WOMAN'S CHARACTER AND PERSONALITY IN BUSINESS

"SHE tried to 'parlorize' my office," was the explanation given by a business man for dismissing a capable assistant. "She was offended if the men failed to pick up the papers she dropt, or to open doors for her, and I saw her use all the coquettish little tricks she'd practise on a man in her own home. She wore slinky, chiffony things, so that she looked helpless when a man was around and he just yearned to do something for her. The joke of it was that she came to me demanding to be paid the same sum as the men clerks in the department—said she believed in equal pay for equal work! Why, the other clerks would have been furious if this helpless little package had been paid the same salary!"

"Rude man," a business girl remarked. "He certainly would have picked up papers for a lady caller in his home. A business woman is just as much a lady, even if she has to work for her living!"

Business is hard for the woman who cleaves to this view-point, because men do make a sharp distinction between their social and their business attitude toward women. In social life man is willing to perform the thousand and one traditional little services prescribed by social usage as a mark of deference to women. But then, the woman's social attitude toward a man differs from her business attitude. Socially she does not ask equality, but thrives on her privileges.

But in business we are demanding equality. If we appear helplessly in need of the attentions and services ordained by social superstition, can we at the same time be regarded as on an equal plane of self-reliance and usefulness? We can not compromise about how much of equality we want—where we want justice to end and privilege to enter. If we are ready to accept the equality program in its entirety, we can not take offense because we are treated like men by men.

The average business man's attitude toward women workers is definitely different from his attitude toward women he meets socially. The business woman has his respect as part of his business organization. But as soon as a woman deliberately "parlorizes" the office by her coquettish mannerisms, conspicuously extravagant clothes, or by exercising abilities usually confined to the courting arena, she brings upon herself the very things she fears.

Lo, the poor business man has been blamed for the result. Purveyors of hectic literature have worn threadbare the theme of the "poor girl caught in the snare of the naughty business man." In justice to the average business man, let it be said that he does not set out to play Don Juan or King Cophetua. Of course, there are exceptions. Unscrupulous men are met in business, just as they are found in some proportion in the "best" circles. But many business women of wide experience, even beautiful ones doing difficult outside work, will testify that the American business man is not prone to "take advantage" of a woman, but is ready to treat her with all the courtesy and directness expected.

The pretty woman is always likely to

be offered flattering attentions from men associates. But an average woman of intelligence is quite capable of freezing an undesired admirer into a state of respectful good sense, without even losing her job in the process. But if it be a case where she can not get rid of the attentions, she can, as a last resort, get rid of the job, for we are not in this country living among bandits. She need never be kissed twice against her will. Moreover, before we utterly condemn the unfortunate rich business man, whose reprehensible attentions to an employee get him into the papers, let us consider certain types of business girls who encourage him while he pursues his way.

Case 1 is Maisie Dorothea, young, beautiful, superbly gowned, who really doesn't have to earn her own living, but has entered business with the hope and intention that it shall prove to be her marriage market. She makes a deliberate attempt to focus attention on her person, either by her clothes, or by an exhibition of thinly disguised, or even frank, coquetry that invites a flirtatious return. Sometimes she succeeds, but not as well as she had hoped.

Then there is an outcry against the ruthless business man who pursued fleeing innocence!

Case 2 is Nellie, the poor working girl. Nellie not only has to work for her own living, but helps to support the family on a tiny salary. Her home is poor, furnished largely with trading-stamp vases, rocking-chairs, lamps and other gimcracks; the kind of cut glass they "give away" with every pound of tea you buy; and leather cushions, created from tabs "given away" with each package of cigarets. Nellie's brother Jim smoked this brand of cigarets fast and furiously for one month at Nellie's request, in order to accumulate the requisite amount of "tabs" for the cushion. Nellie has been reared on the "something-for-nothing" idea.

Nellie can pay her way to the "movies" occasionally, or perhaps even to a dance with girl friends. She can't afford many other pleasures. Yes, there may be public libraries, public concerts, art galleries and lectures to which she can go, but Nellie doesn't care for that sort of thing. Her taste has not been educated in these directions. Now it happens one fine day that O. Henry's "Piggy" approaches with flattering invitations—apparently impelled thereto by her irresistible good looks. Nellie sees in "Piggy" merely a "good thing," is offered theater tickets, dinners, taxicab rides, luxuries she could never afford, apparently for nothing. She accepts them, without expecting to give a return.

What does a young man do in the same position? If he yearns for smart dinners, evenings at the theater, and automobile rides on his $8 per week, he saves up until he has "the price," and then he has his evening of reckless joy—at his own expense. But Nellie does not "smell a rat" in the something-for-nothing proposition. She accepts it, responding to the same instinct that moved her mother to buy a kind of tea she didn't want, in order to get "for nothing" a piece of cut glass, which she doesn't need.

Eventually Nellie finds herself launched on the primrose path of discreditable comfort, and when some day she achieves a place as Case No. So-and-so in the report of a sociological commission, we ask in pity, "Why, oh why?" Nellie had a safe home. She had a job. Tho poor, she was decently comfortable. She had friends and some sources of amusement. "If the men didn't come after us and offer us things!" she sobs in self-defense. Why didn't Nellie have the training and the backbone to resist the lure of "something-for-nothing?" Why hasn't she the intelligence to perceive that the "something-for-nothing" offer should be regarded as a danger signal to "stop, look and listen?"

Something for nothing is worth just the price—worth just nothing. A bargain is inevitably costly when it means time wasted, wear and tear on nervous energy, or a weakening of the moral fiber. Nellie doesn't regard her ability to get something for nothing as anything more than a harmless foible to be smiled at. But, once make her understand that it isn't a girlish pastime, but has elemental connection with many of the real disasters in a woman's life, and she will be more careful about putting herself in a dependent position toward gentlemen seeking diversion. Nellie needs, more than anything, to be educated in the principle that everything in life has its price, and to have instilled in her a true sense of values.

There are differing opinions on the subject of whether business associates make desirable social companions. In some of the large organizations where "welfare" plans are operated, may be found entertainment rooms in the plant itself—reading-rooms, rest-rooms, auditoriums for meetings and dances, all to encourage social relations among the employees. This is a life-saver to the woman who is working in a strange city and has no other means of making friends for her leisure hours. Where the organization is so large that employees do not meet during business hours and hardly know each other in a business way, many delightful friendships are formed.

But in the average small business, employees will not find it desirable to extend their acquaintances into social life. There is too much tendency to "talk shop" in the hours spent away from business. The business woman needs to get completely away from work at the end of the day. She can not relax or be refreshed if the thoughts of the working day are still dinned into her tired mind. Other interests and other people are stimulating and more enjoyable. Then, too, the meeting of employees in the intimacy of social life may result in the spread of mischievous, or garbled, comments. Confidential bits of information that would never have been breathed inside the office are discust in the privacy of the social circle—and circulated thereafter.

There was a time when the problem of "how to entertain a business man" was the one bar to a woman's gaining an important position. The '"out-of-town" customers expected to be entertained at luncheon or dinner when they visited the office, and, of course, it would be embarrassing, and might be offensive, to some men to be entertained by a woman. But conditions have changed. In the first place, there is less entertaining for business reasons. Self-respecting buyers object because it savors of bribery. Many organizations have definite rules against it. However, when it is expedient to entertain a business man (and some still feel that a new deal can best be discust over the luncheon or dinner table) the modern woman is prepared to meet the situation gracefully.

She may be a member of a woman's club, where men guests can be asked to dine.

Then, of course, she can be as gracious a hostess as tho she were entertaining in her own home. If not, she can make arrangements beforehand with the manager of a good dining-place to have a table reserved, and dinner served without a check being presented at the end. The presenting of the check is the one possible embarrassment in these days when a man is supposed to pay for a woman's entertainment in public, and not women for men. The bill is simply forwarded to the woman's office next day and promptly paid. Several business firms employing one or two women executives have a permanent account at some high-class hotel near the office, so that these women can have men as luncheon or dinner guests at any time without any possible embarrassment.

Gone are the days when a striped blouse, a stiff, mannish collar, a four-in-hand tie, an ugly rainy-day skirt, were considered the only proper regalia for the business woman. But are we advancing when we adopt in their stead the cold-inviting, transparent flimsies in blouse and hose, and the high-heeled, unhygienic pumps? It is quite possible to look neat and well-drest in business by wearing either simply made, opaque blouses of good material, or several one-piece gowns with low collars and sleeves reaching slightly below the elbow for comfort, which will always look dignified and keep neater than the blouse and skirt.

One business woman who lives in the suburbs, and therefore finds it necessary to wear her "best clothes" to the office when she has a social engagement in town for the evening, has solved a problem for many business women. She has invented what she calls an "office coat for business women." It is a black silk, long-sleeved coat, with simple lines and no trimming. She wears this coat over her gown all day and so keeps her dress beneath fresh and unspotted for the evening. She also keeps concealed in this way the gown that would appear entirely too fussy for business.

How much of her income shall the business woman spend for clothes? The sum will vary according to the income and position, but it is a safe plan to stick to a fixt percentage. The sums spent will automatically keep pace with the advance in position and necessity for wearing better clothes.

As will be seen in the suggested budgets in the following chapter, about 15 per cent. is a general average. In cities this proportion may seem small, because it has come to pass that women who go to business have endeavored to imitate the "society" woman in their apparel. One business man declared that he never paid a woman more than $25 a week, because that sum covered her necessities and, even if she was worth more, there was no sense in paying it to her, as she would only spend it on more furbelows and clothes, clothes, clothes. Outside of clothes, women preserve a curious indifference toward their physical well-being. This is illustrated especially in the matter of food.

What is the average lunch of the busy business man? Even if it's a "quick lunch," it is a substantial one—a sandwich, milk and pie, or a savory stew, or a bowl of milk and crackers. Men are more likely to err in consuming too substantial foods, and consuming them too quickly. But a woman's "quick lunch," likely as not, is a dish of ice cream, or some pastry and coffee supplemented by all or part of a pound of candy nibbled during the afternoon.

At four o'clock the busy worker wonders why she feels sleepy, or weak and dispirited, and perhaps attributes it to overwork. As a matter of fact, if she had been fortified with a well-balanced luncheon, and worked in a well-ventilated room with correct lighting and seating arrangements, there would be no reason why she should feel any fatigue after four or five hours' work. Any woman, even without dietetic training, can know enough to select a correct luncheon for herself. The outdoor worker consuming muscular energy, needs muscle-building elements, the proteids, meat, fish, eggs, beans, peas, nuts. The indoor, or sedentary, worker needs the fats, starches and sugars, which are energy producers. An outdoor, muscular worker can safely consume a large quantity of food at midday, but her sedentary office sister needs to eat sparingly. Below are given a few typical "balanced" menus, which may serve as a guide to a correct selection of a luncheon:

FOR THE GIRL IN THE OFFICE—A SEDENTARY WORKER

Tomato Purée Brown Bread
Chocolate Layer Cake Milk

Cheese Sandwiches Boiled Rice
Ice Cream

Egg Salad Toast
Hot or Cold Chocolate

Baked Beans Brown Bread
Graham Crakers Lemonade

Vegetable Soup Sardine Sandwich
Baked Apple

Omelet Creamed Potato
Sliced Pineapple

Clam Chowder Crackers
Rice Pudding

THE AMBITIOUS WOMAN IN BUSINESS

FOR THE WOMAN DOING OUTSIDE, OR MUSCULAR, WORK

(*Winter*)

Cream of Tomato Soup
Lamb Chop Baked Sweet Potato
Layer Cake

Beefsteak Pie
Sliced Oranges Cookies

Baked Oysters
Tomato Salad Baked Potato
Custard

(*Summer*)

Egg Salad Scalloped Potatoes
Muffins and Marmalade
Lemonade

Spaghetti and Cheese
Strawberry Shortcake Iced Cocoa

Baked Beans Creamed Carrots
Sliced Pineapple

Cream of Corn Soup
Omelet Brown Bread
Sliced Bananas with Lemon Juice

These are simply suggestions of suitable menus. Any one can select from the menu of the average business eating-house the right kind of nutritious meal, instead of leaving the selection to the unguided caprice of an immediate appetite. If there is no convenient restaurant which offers the right kind of food, it is far better for a group of girls to arrange to bring their luncheon from home, and the right luncheon, than to accept such food as a low-grade restaurant tries to impose on them. The woman who puts into active practise the principles of good nutrition will have no more desire for a luncheon of ice cream and a charlotte russe, than for a luncheon of oyster stew, chicken croquets, macaroni and custard pie!

Loss of appetite is usually caused, either by poorly chosen food, or by a habit of sitting down immediately to a meal after several hours of strenuous work. It is a good plan first to rest for ten or fifteen minutes before sitting down to eat. The fatigue of the day culminates just about when the tired business woman arrives home after her journey from the office. She may feel no appetite for the substantial foods her body needs, but that is a temporary condition. If she throws herself on a couch or bed for about fifteen minutes, relaxing every muscle and freeing her mind from work or worry, she will find an awakened appetite.

Above all, the cares of business should not be taken home. Lock them up in your desk at night. The important point for a woman to remember, especially at the beginning of her career, is to conserve her energy. To know how to relax is as important as to know how to work! Even the business man who feels he can not afford a few weeks' vacation will, nevertheless, allow himself an afternoon off to see a baseball game, or will go off on a few days' fishing trip, and he is all the better for such healthy self-indulgence. Men seem to heed more the call of the great outdoors. It requires much will-power for a woman to cling to the habit of daily exercise.

The easiest way to overcome mental inertia toward exercise is to make a hobby of some special sport—swimming, or tennis, or golf—or to join an athletic club where social companionship will be possible during exercise. If the body is exercised, it becomes your well-disciplined servant; but if neglected, it becomes a tyrannical, unpleasant master. If there is not time two or three hours a week for some special exercise, there is time for five or ten minutes of exercise immediately on rising in the morning and just before retiring at night. It is much better to take five minutes regularly each day than to resolve to take thirty minutes, do it once or twice, and then drop it altogether! A warm bath, not exceeding five minutes in duration, is an excellent aid to peaceful sleep if taken just before retiring. In the morning, a cold rub is an excellent stimulant, but the cold bath can be taken only when the body responds quickly—not by a woman inclined to be anemic, or who takes a chill easily.

Plenty of fresh air—both during night and during day—is an excellent insurance against the ills that come to the strenuous worker. Outdoor sleeping is an ideal health-guard for a woman doing sedentary work inside an office during the day. If you have a porch that can be screened, or a bedroom that can be projected outdoors by rebuilding a few windows, press it into service as a sleeping porch. The expense will pay for itself many times in a wonderful increase in health.

Lack of fresh air contributes to the office woman's ills more than she sometimes realizes. It is an unfathomable mystery why so many women, who have spent their leisure hours in typical city diversions—dances, theaters, card parties and other indoor amusements—should so often elect to spend two or three weeks' of summer vacation at a fashionable seaside or mountain resort where exactly the same city pleasures prevail and the same type of city people are encountered.

The ideal vacation is the vacation that gives the most fresh air, and the most change—not necessarily the one that permits the greatest amount of sleep or lounging. Ocean travel is less costly than vacations at many fashionable resorts which business women patronize, and it is far more health-building. Better still are a few weeks of camping, roughing it in some neck o' the woods, where all diversions are outdoor sports. It should not be a luxurious summer camp, fitted with city conveniences, but some rough shack or tent, where the vacationist who has worked with her brain the year round will have to work with her hands instead, doing the quick, rude housekeeping of camp life.

The use of her hands is a valuable faculty often lost to the woman brainworker. One often observes the most amusing lack of physical coordination in the successful business woman of thirty, who has never exerted herself in any direction outside her daily work. For this reason, study of the homemaking arts—cooking, cleaning, planning and decorating a home—is a splendid diversion as well as an education for a business woman. It calls into play other muscles and cultivates latent esthetic tastes as well.

IX

THE BUSINESS WOMAN'S FINANCES

WHAT does the business woman who supports only herself do with her salary? It would seem that the woman who earns $15 or $20 a week, or more, could live comfortably and save some of her salary, but investigation has shown time and again that the saving habit is rare among business women. Many reasons are offered. First, that it costs her a great deal to live, or that her position requires that she dress well, and the cost of clothing cuts considerably into her income. "Incidentals," too, are a large item which she can not account for in detail.

An insurance statistician has declared that business women do not save money unless they are in the class that earn from $6 to $9 per week. Such girls sometimes have been induced to take out easy industrial insurance which costs only a few cents per week. Altho their savings are tiny, they do save something. Trained nurses and school teachers are two other classes of wage-earning women who save. But, generally speaking, the business woman's extravagance seems to mount with her income! "I haven't time to examine into the safety of investments," declared one business woman who admitted that on her $3,000 salary she had not saved money, had not a single investment to her name. One banking house, recognizing the fact that women, even experienced business women, are reluctant to invest in stocks and bonds, went to the trouble of installing a special woman's department, presided over by a woman, in order to encourage women in making discriminating investments.

It is not enough to have an instinct for saving, or to be naturally economical. It is absolutely necessary for the far-sighted business woman to save systematically, if her savings are to amount to anything. Some business concerns help their employees to develop the saving habit by establishing a "bank" in the plant itself. One department store, for example, operated a bank under the name of the "Employees' Savings and Loan Association." Their plan was to sell shares of stock in the bank at $25 per share. Deposits applicable on this share of stock had to be made each week on a given day. Those failing to make a deposit on that day were fined at the rate of 2 cents per share, this fine going to the general fund that increased the dividends. Two objects were achieved by this plan; one, the formation of habits of regular saving; the other, making it unnecessary for needy employees to borrow from loan sharks, since they could withdraw cash from their own account, plus ten dollars which could be paid back later in weekly or monthly instalments.

Where there is no outside incentive to saving, the business woman herself can establish methods of regular saving by spending her income according to a budgeted plan. That is what progressive business firms do; they spend according to prearranged "appropriations." The prudent housewife arranges her expenditures according to a fixt budget, and saves money in the same manner. It is absolutely necessary to include a percentage of savings in a budget, or there will not be any savings.

Women who have homes of their own can probably adapt the "ideal budget" for family use, which is approximately, as follows:

BUDGET FOR FOUR PEOPLE ON A $20 PER WEEK INCOME

	Per cent
Food	25
Rent	20
Operating (light, heat, service)	15
Clothing	20
Amusement, education, etc.	10
Savings	10

Of course, there are variations in some of these percentages according to income, locality, standards of living, position, and other factors. The *percentage* required for food is higher for an income smaller than $20 and lower for a higher one. The percentage for rent and operating remains about the same for any income, the amount so spent keeping pace with the decreased or increased income.

The business woman who boards pays rent, food and operating expenses in one lump sum, plus another special lunch and carfare item. It is possible that her expenses here will amount to somewhat more than the amounts spent by the woman who keeps house. The householder pays cost price for food, rent and operating. But the business woman who boards pays all of these items, plus a profit to the individual who boards her.

Below are given some suggested budgets for the business woman with a fixt salary. If she works on some basis where her income is fluctuating, her budget is determined by averaging her monthly income for the past one or two years, and apportioning her budget on this average:

SUGGESTED BUDGETS FOR BUSINESS WOMEN WHO BOARD

	$10 Weekly Salary		
Board (rent, operating, food) ..	50%	or	$ 5.00
Carfare and lunch	15%		1.50
Clothes	15%		1.50
Amusement, education, etc.....	10%		1.00
Savings	10%		1.00

Savings a year on $10 income, $52.

	$15 Weekly Salary		
Board (rent, operating, food)	50%	or	$ 7.50
Carfare and lunch	15%		2.25
Clothes	15%		2.25
Amusement, education, etc.	10%		1.50
Savings	10%		1.50

Savings a year on $15 income, $78.

	$25 Weekly Salary		
Board (rent, operating, food)	40%	or	$10.00
Carfare and lunch	15%		3.75
Clothes	15%		3.75
Education, amusement, etc.	10%		2.50
Savings	20%		5.00

Savings a year on $25 income, $260.

	$50 Weekly Salary		
Board (rent, operating, food)	40%	or	$20.00
Carfare and lunch	10%		5.00
Clothes	15%		7.50
Amusement, education, etc.	10%		5.00
Savings	25%		12.50

Savings a year on $50 income, $650.

Unusual expenses, such as gifts, doctor's bills, etc., are paid for out of the "amusement and education" division. These budgets lend themselves to adjustments. Because of her business position, the business woman often finds it necessary to spend more money on clothes than her actual needs require, or she may have to entertain, or there may be other factors which make it desirable to depart from the percentage fixt above.

Many business girls throw up their hands in horror at the thought of clothing themselves on $78 a year. But if you have a $10 salary, you must cut expenses right and left. It is better to cut clothing expenses than to starve the body by trying to achieve the impossible in an effort to save on food. Food is the last place in which to save, because above all things the body must be well nourished to keep in health.

Here is a detailed statement of the clothing expenses of a business woman having a $15 per week income. As some of the articles were worn for more than one season, the cost is in some cases spread over two or three seasons. The average total spent for clothing in this case was $120 per year. The girl who has only $78 a year can use this as a guide, because many of the items on the list are not absolute necessities. It is possible to cut them out if the income does not permit anything beyond actual needs. For example, the girl with a $10 a week income can eliminate such luxuries as a silk petticoat, or a $10 hat, or a $20 frock, or silk stockings. These are not unreasonable extravagances for the girl who can afford them, but they are absurd expenses for the girl with a $10 income. She can buy neat, good-looking apparel for smaller sums, and it is on just such costly accessories as silk hose, fine hats and party frocks that she can save. It is not wise to save on the daily business suit, or on any garment that is bought for wear. A well-made tailored suit of good fabric may come high, but it is durable, will wear for more than one season, and always looks well. This itemized statement of clothing expenses may not be ideal for all business women of the same income, but it at least shows how the apportionment for clothing can be divided sensibly:

Suits, coats, waists, gowns:	*Original Cost*	*Length of Wear (Years)*	*Average Yearly Cost*
Tailored suit	$ 30.00	2	$ 15.00
Warm coat	18.00	3	6.00
Waterproof coat	6.00	3	2.00
Tailored waists, 3 @ $2	6.00	2	3.00
Silk waist	5.00	2	2.50
Thin summer waists, 2	2.00	1	2.00
Sweater	5.00	4	1.25
Evening dress	20.00	2	10.00
Wool dress for winter	16.00	2	8.00
Light summer dress	10.00	2	5.00

Hats, gloves, shoes:	*Original Cost*	*Length of Wear (Years)*	*Average Yearly Cost*
Summer hat, daily wear ..	2.50	1	2.50
Summer hat, best	4.00	1	4.00
Winter hat, daily wear ...	3.00	1	3.00
Winter hat, best	5.00	2	2.50
Gloves (warm mitts)....	1.00	2	.50
Gloves, chamois	1.00	1	1.00
Gloves, kid, 1 pair......	1.25	1	1.25
Gloves, silk, 1 pair, elbow	1.50	1	1.50
Gaiters	1.00	1	1.00
Rubbers	.75	1	.75
Shoes, winter, house	1.50	2	.75
Shoes, winter, heavy	4.00	1	4.00
Shoes, summer, house ...	1.00	1	1.00
Shoes, summer	3.50	1	3.50
Shoes, dress	6.00	2	3.00
Underwear and Sundries:			
Corsets, 1 pair..........	3.00	1	3.00
Kimona, summer	2.50	2	1.25
Kimona, winter	6.00	4	1.50
Nightgowns, summer, 3..	3.00	2	1.50
Nightgowns, winter, 3...	4.50	3	1.50
Combinations, 2 suits....	3.00	2	1.50
Union suits, summer, 3 pr.	3.00	1	3.00
Union suits, winter, 3 pr..	6.00	2	3.00
Stockings, summer, 3 pr.	1.00	1	1.00
Stockings, winter, 3 pr....	1.50	1	1.50
Stockings, silk, 2 pair...	3.00	2	1.50
Umbrella	2.00	2	1.00
Sundries, like belts, veils, handkerchiefs, aprons, neckwear, etc	10.00		10.00
	$203.50	Cost per year	$116.25

Such a division of items presupposes care in the handling of clothes. The main economy here is in the use of the same garments for more than one season. Altho some of the items may appear large as initial expenditures, nevertheless they are spent in the interest of far-sighted economy. The heavy expense of clothing for some women is not due to the fact that they must buy so much, but because they buy so unwisely. They purchase a 98-cent flimsy that will not wear longer than a month, when for $1.50 they might have obtained something more substantial that would have worn for two seasons. Another source of waste in clothing is the habit of haphazard buying —picking up a veil, or a blouse, or some hose, not because it is needed, but because "it's such a bargain." When the business woman goes shopping, she might do well to stick in her purse a card bearing Franklin's advice, "Never buy anything you don't need because it is cheap!" It might keep her from falling over the brink at the last moment!

A great help to the business woman in adhering to her budget is keeping accounts. In a little book she can enter her income, and keep accurate record of all her expenditures for food and clothing, and an itemized record of the many little leaks which she would otherwise have dismissed from her mind under the blanket charge of "Incidentals." An account book will act, not only as a reminder to keep within the budget she has prescribed for herself, but also will help her to equalize expenses. If her account book shows that last month her expenses exceeded the budget allowance by $10 she will know that she must plan this month to cut her expenses that much, or distribute the extra expense over a required period. Best of all, keeping accounts will give her a more businesslike attitude in regard to her own finances. Just as in business the prudent man is ever on the alert to keep down expenses and cut unnecessary costs, so will the business woman who keeps accounts hold a watchful eye over her own expenses. She will also administer her finances with a purpose in mind, and not squander her all unthinkingly, without regard to the future.

The efficient business woman should possess, by the time she is thirty years old, (1) A piece of land on which she can build; or her own house paid for in full, cr in part; (2) An endowment insurance policy to safeguard her old age; (3) a small bank account from which she can draw ready cash in case of need. Possession of these three does not necessarily require a large capital. They are necessary for the self-supporting woman, even if she thinks there is no likelihood of her being self-supporting all her days. If she begins, as early in her career as possible, to pay for a home, she has the security of a home that will always be hers. If she does not desire to live in it alone, she can rent it and so receive some income from that source. An initial investment of a few hundred dollars is sometimes sufficient to secure a modest piece of land, and the desire to own it, free and clear, is a spur to greater saving.

Endowment insurance is not a burden, costing only from $40 to $50 per thousand dollars, approximately, on a twenty-year plan, and sometimes less, depending on the individual's age, health, and the rates of various companies. The policy matures at the time a business woman is of middle age, and is always a welcome nest egg. Other types of policies bear an accident clause, whereby the full amount of the policy is paid to the holder if she is mentally or physically incapacitated. The business woman who is far-sighted enough to anticipate any possible condition in her future, and to prepare for it, need therefore not fear that she will ever be a dependent invalid. It does not require exorbitant sums to provide for herself—simply a little judicious foresight, and the strength of will to save regularly, no matter what her circumstances.

Before investing savings in stocks or bonds the business woman should have complete information about the investment. It is wise to have a trustworthy broker, but it is more desirable that the business woman should herself know the law and practise regarding such investments, as well as the facts about her particular investment. Women are often an easy prey of wild-cat speculations promising fabulous returns, simply because they do not understand the mechanism of investment and speculation. Stocks that are not known or quoted on the exchange are always more or less doubtful—probably as speculative as mining stocks in unheard-of districts. Unless you are thoroughly familiar with the company, its solvency, possible market, possible profits, and most important of all, with the integrity of the officials, an investment in its stock is a questionable proposition. The lot of a minority stockholder in the new corporation is not a profitable one.

Of course, the bonds of a government, or of profit-producing corporations are almost always safe, because these bear interest regularly, and bondholders have claims on the property of the organization in advance of stockholders. Stockholders receive dividends from their investment only when there are dividends, or profits. Before making any investments the business woman would do well to read some of the books on the subject appended to this volume, so that she may have a basis for making judicious decisions.

X

HOME AND MARRIAGE AND THE BUSINESS WOMAN

CAN a woman have a career, a home and a family at one and the same time? A man who has a business career, a home, and a family is conceded generally to be living a normal life. But only a small band of feminists and "radicals" believe that a woman can have these three interests and yet retain health and feminine charm, and be perfectly normal. The voice of the majority says to the modern woman, "You can have either a career or a family; you can not have both." Let us examine impartially the facts which support these positions before allying ourselves definitely with either party.

(1) Is it necessary that a woman shall have a business, home and family like a man? Or, to put it differently, is a woman so limited, or privileged by nature, that she ought to be satisfied with only half of

three life interests? Does the normal woman really want business, home and family simultaneously?

(2) Is it beneficial or harmful for a woman to endeavor to "swing" a career and a family at the same time? Does she work an injustice, either to the family or to business when she divides her time between both, as a man does?

(3) Even if we admit that it is desirable for woman to have three interests like a man, how is it possible or practical under present industrial conditions?

First then, is it necessary, from an economic standpoint, that the woman who wants to marry, have a home and family, shall also have a career which yields financial support? In a previous chapter it was shown that the average man's income is under $20 a week, and his statistical family consists of four or five persons; therefore, his unmarried adult daughters consider it desirable and necessary that they should be self-supporting. But must daughter Jane continue to be self-supporting when she marries? Won't some John desire to support her?

We will assume that John is not one of the very exceptional young men who have succeeded at a tender age; nor is he in the small group of young men who have inherited wealth. He is just an average young man at an age when he wants to marry. Now, he may have the chivalrous impulse of protection toward Jane, but it is undeniable that the average young man, in the early years of his career (which is also the time when he wants to marry), finds it difficult to secure the living which the world owes him.

Here is a curious and significant fact. The average young woman who reaches her high peak of business success between the ages of 20 and 30, probably earns more than the average young man of that age. Of course, Jane does not realize this great distinction. As she has fixt no high goal for business success, she has reached the maximum of her earning power at 23 or 26 years of age. At that maximum she will stick. John, at the same time, is earning much less, mainly because he is doing the preparatory work for an eventual high goal.

Jane feels very superior as a $20 a week

stenographer, while John, altho three years her senior, is only a struggling young law clerk with a $12 salary. Jane is a practical young woman, and the money question is discust during their courtship days. They decide that they want to be "sensible," and so, if they love each other very much, they agree to "wait" until John's salary is big enough to take care of both—and they wait until the zest of early courtship is almost gone. Or perhaps Jane has been spoiled irremediably by the comforts her $20 buys when she spends it all on herself. John is too proud to suggest that she make a sacrifice. He knows it will be a long, long time before he can keep her in such comfort. So they separate, keep their respective pride and comfort, and lose each other.

After a few years Jane gets so self-centered, and so much married to her individualistic habits, that marriage with any man is a sacrifice she refuses to make. Now, if John is too poor to take care of two people single-handed, why on earth shouldn't Jane help him by continuing her work after marriage? Two people can live more cheaply than one if both work. To be perfectly just to the modern Jane, that is what she wants to do. She isn't in any doubt as to whether she shall choose work or marriage—she wants both, and for several reasons. One reason is that she wants to be with John now. She loves him, is interested in him, and life is half empty without him.

The second reason is that she realizes that her interest in work is an integral part of her life, aside even from its economic returns. Divorce from daily work has become for her about as pleasant a prospect as having an amputated limb would be. But, suppose that John is able to support her amply immediately on marriage. What happens? Jane finds herself suddenly transferred from the stimulation of daily business, where she was in frequent contact with keen minds, and where adventure and change lurked constantly, to quiet, solitary affairs within the four walls of her home. If Jane was the type of woman to whom business is a temporary purgatory, to be endured only until she had reached the heaven of matrimony, she would be content. Even if she was of a higher type, of a more ambitious sort, and altogether normal, she would find a keen and novel interest in keeping house for John. But if she has ever amounted to much in business, there comes, after honeymoon days are over, an intense void, an aching loneliness for the habits of many years of business occupation. It is a perfectly natural reaction which any man interested in his business, and who has had to be separated from that business, can understand. It might astonish many husbands to know that their wives, altho comfortably installed, spend considerable time during the first year after marriage, secretly seeking "part-time" jobs. It is happy young brides who often answer seductive advertisements offering to "pay $20 a week for your work in spare time." Indeed, the yearning for business habits is not confined entirely to the woman whose business life has been especially interesting. A pretty factory girl once actually confest to an adoring young husband, soon after the honeymoon, that she was miserably lonely and unhappy in their cozy little flat. She yearned to get back to paper-box making and the pleasant chatter of the girls!

And then there is Julia, who lived in a mental turmoil during a five-year engagement because she couldn't give up Paul and stick to her job, and wouldn't give up her job and stick to Paul. Julia had entered business because it was necessary for her to earn her own living. Gradually she grew deeply interested in business, as she became more proficient, and saw that business was not merely monotonous labor, but that it offered the stimulation of interesting mental contact, with many incentives for rewards and promotion for special effort. Then Paul came and she wanted very much to marry him. But she rebelled at the idea of ending her business career, just when it was beginning to yield the results of years of uphill work, and at the thought of discarding hard-fought-for knowledge of business now marketable at a good price to enter the new occupation of housekeeping in which she was an incapable amateur.

Why should marriage affect Julia's work any more than it affected Paul's? What did love have to do with housekeeping, anyhow? She thought she would perish if she had to give up her daily mental combats with keen minds in business, in order to combat daily and alone with recalcitrant recipes and scrub-brush monotony. She was a mind, not a muscle. She had neither training nor desire for housework. She could use part of the salary she earned to pay a competent housekeeper to do the housework.

But Paul declared that he loved her too much to see her out in a cold and cruel business world after they were married. A home and family would keep her sufficiently occupied, he said. He would be proud to have her share his own business interests, and give him the benefit of her experience and counsel. But Julia was an independent person. She did not want to get her business interest vicariously because she had spent a long time building a perfectly good business interest of her own.

Paul's mother thought it was Julia's duty to devote herself completely to Paul's comfort, and not leave what should be a task of love to a hireling. Anyway, it was extravagant for two people to have a servant. Julia's mother said that woman's place was in the home, and Julia would find plenty of things to keep her busy soon enough. And all of Julia's and Paul's relatives insinuated that it was too bad Paul couldn't afford to support Julia! Finally, she didn't marry Paul and she didn't give up her job, and two strong-minded, desirable people who loved each other lived each a fractional life.

As the majority were against Julia's position, let us consider their reasons. First, her plan would have been unjust to her husband, because she could not have made a good, comfortable home for him if she divided her time between home and business. Secondly, she would have ruined her health if she had attempted it. Housekeeping, they insisted, was an occupation in itself, sufficient to keep a woman at work "from sun to sun." Thirdly, it wasn't practical. She would have had to be in her office from nine to six o'clock each day, and as she had to travel from business to the home, this meant an absence of ten hours a day from home. How could she do this if she had young children, and of course, Julia wanted children? The trouble was that Julia's relatives argued from tradition instead of reason. Julia, on the other hand, was short-sighted in regarding her business as a separate entity instead of planning it in its relation to her whole life. The more they argued, the larger to her did her job loom up in importance and desirableness.

The argument often advanced that a home requires all a wife's time and attention as soon as she marries, is based on the traditional idea of a home—the home of yesterday, which was really a factory. But the home of to-day is more an office type of home, requiring more administrative than mechanical ability. Modern housekeeping, with its labor-saving machinery, is a comparatively simple process, especially for a family of two people. Julia's indifferent housekeeping was not needed in the home. Even if they had lived in a large house and she had replaced herself with a trained worker, she could have kept the reins of home management in her own hands, and the results would have been better than if she had attempted to do all the manual work herself. The responsibilities of the home in addition to those of business could hardly have "ruined her health." In fact, diversion of interest has proved a definite relaxation to business women.

As far as housekeeping itself was concerned, Julia was right and her relatives were wrong. But would it not have been unjust to her husband for her to have had such a large outside interest? In actual practise this does not seem to be the case. What man would not prefer above the woman having pots-and-pans interests, the wife whose ever-moving interests kept pace with his own? The more interests she had, the more companionable would she be. The greater her intelligence in work, the more intelligent and discriminating would she be in making a comfortable home. In fact, the ethical advantages incident to Julia's continuation in business were so much more Paul's advantages than Julia's that it is amazing he did not insist that Julia continue to work outside the home until children came.

But Paul's social position had to be considered. What would people say about him for permitting his wife to share in the support of the home? There would be aspersions on his chivalry. Perhaps, even, his business solvency would be questioned! Besides, he would feel that he was not doing his full duty as a husband, if he did not personally and individually shoulder the economic responsibility of the home.

The attitude of Paul and his type toward the economic aspects of marriage is most difficult to understand when they attempt to be ethical. There is no criticism of the lovely, well-bred young women who marry, in cold blood, men for whom they have no sincere affection, simply because they want to be supported or to have a few more luxuries. In love stories in popular magazines, the ubiquitous theme is a woman's method in securing marriage with a man of wealth. A conservative woman's magazine will appeal to its readers with a fine democratic tale of some noble society girl who makes a sacrifice for love's sake, and marries a poor man with only $3,000 a year!

As long as marriage means financial dependence to a woman, there will always be a just basis of questioning her motives in marriage. It must be gall and wormwood to a man who married his wife for pure love of her, to discover that she married him—as she would have married any one else if she had had the chance—for three meals a day. If we could remove the economic factor from marriage, almost all marriages would be love marriages and quite naturally. There would be no need for any other kind. Supposing Julia shares the economic responsibilities of the home in due proportion. Will not Paul have a just pride in this proof that he was selected on the basis of his human qualities and not for his property? When she cleaves to him, will he not feel assured that it is because she finds him a lovable individual, and not because she wants to use him as a bank? The masculine purse-strings are a chain and harness which bind the woman long after love has ceased to hold her. To men, marriage has meant the romance of an exalted chase; but too often the glory has been taken out of it because of woman's attitude: that marriage is a "gainful occupation." Romance was a desirable incidental, but the main issue considered was: is the man an "eligible"; is he able to support me in good style so that my friends will think I have made a "good match?"

When Julia shares the economic responsibilities, as well as the joys, of home life with him, Paul gains the tremendous ethical advantage of marrying on a basis of mutual love, self-respect and equality. There is another psychical advantage which both share. When Julia has business interests and Paul has business interests, they grow together, and thus avoid the familiar tragedy of the self-made business man rising way out of sight of his devoted wife. She has bound herself so exclusively to him that no independent interest has ever entered her life. Her very clinging devotion, instead of making her more attractive, has arrested her development and she can give her husband nothing in exchange for his wealth of knowledge and ideas. And even the vainest man wearies after a time of a diet of perpetual adoration from a weak creature whose bread and butter depends on her adoration! It is the woman with an independent business, or a professional interest, who has the capacity for stimulating companionship, and the ability to exchange ideas of value.

But what sort of home atmosphere will there be when the "tired business husband" comes home to the "tired business wife?" That is one of the frequent arguments against the married woman in business.

In actual practise we see that in such families there is generally more of a tendency to seek recreations mutually agreeable. There is more truth than we suspect in the old jest about the worn and weary business man being dragged away from his comfortable fireside by a home-biding wife. It is true she greets him at night in a lovely fresh costume, a rose in her hair and a delight to his eye. Having spent the day within the four walls of her home she eagerly looks forward to her husband's return home so that they may go away for the evening—to the dance, theater, or some other diversion. But to the man battling in business all day, home is his diversion. He desires to relax in the home atmosphere, and it is one of the common causes of "uncongeniality" and divorce that his wife insists on his joining her in evening amusements for which he is too tired, altho she has been resting during the day, in anticipation of the evening recreations she wants.

On the other hand, the woman who has

spent most of her day, like her husband, in business, will feel exactly as he does. The quiet companionship in the evening, developing together cultural interests outside their business thoughts will afford both the relaxation they desire. Unlike many housewives who fill their husband's evening hour with complaints and woes of the day, the business wife realizes what the battle of business is, and wisely makes sure that the evening hours together are undisturbed by tales of wo.

So far then, Julia's plan of combining work and marriage redounds to the advantage of all concerned, ethically, psychically and financially. Her conceptions of equality—of having both a home and a business as her husband has—are not only possible of execution, but highly desirable. But, there is a rock on which Julia's ideals are bound to split, and that is the child. Julia wants children as much as Paul does. But the greater part of the burden of the child inevitably will fall on Julia. In this there can be no equality. Extreme feminists come forward with instances of teacher-mothers returning to their class-rooms a few weeks after the birth of a child. But these are isolated instances, and physically impossible for the average woman. Even if they were possible, they are admittedly inadvisable. Physicians agree that for the well-being of the child it should receive its mother's care during infancy.

"But surely," it is argued, "a competent nurse would be much better for the child than an inexperienced mother." It is doubtful whether Julia can afford to add a competent nurse to her *ménage*. Also, unlike housekeeping, which is better performed by a trained worker than by an inexperienced wife, most of the duties of motherhood, by reason of their emotional basis, can not be delegated to a hired substitute during the child's early infancy. Even if Julia could afford a high-class nurse, could she, after spending a sleepless night with the baby's croup, hand the ailing infant over to a nurse in the morning at eight o'clock, and blithely go off to her office and forget all about it? What kind of work would she be able to do during weeks when the three babies all had the measles? Would she be satisfied (as fathers are) to look at them for a minute night and morning?

Yes, there are widowed mothers who do this because they must. There are also society mothers who are that "strange, beautiful lady" who visits the nursery occasionally. But Julia is not a society woman, nor is she a widowed mother. She is just a normal girl, who yearns to have a happy, well-rounded life—marriage, motherhood, plus a career. She recognizes that she will not be a complete individual in the biggest sense if one of these is denied her. Yet, how can she keep her work, and take on the further cares and responsibilities of motherhood?

Bear in mind also this point: Julia is the type of conscientious business woman who has thrown herself whole-heartedly into making herself a business success, making the common error of neglecting other phases of her development. What wonder is it, then, that she hesitates to snap off suddenly the ties that bind her to a work in which she is interested and is competent, in order to concentrate herself on the duties of a home where she is ignorant and incompetent? So the solution of her problem probably lies in a program of preparedness. Let marriage be a part of her life-program;

let her anticipate it and prepare for it, just as she prepares for an occupation, with these reservations:

(1) Before marriage, to regard business as a vocation demanding the highest and most serious effort toward a big goal. But practise homemaking arts as an avocation.
(2) After marriage, work until babies come, when home and children are to be the vocation demanding the highest efforts and concentration. But some time should be devoted to premarital business interests, as an avocation.
(3) When the children are grown, complete time and attention may again be given to business.

The second item on this program presents several difficulties, even tho it seems a practical solution of the modern business woman's problem of living. While professional women, like the painter or literary worker, can continue work and yet remain in the home with supervising eye, business hours make it impossible for the woman with young children to continue work in store, office or factory. There are few "part-time" jobs in business which could be filled dependably by a woman who had small children to care for at home.

Therefore, there are two alternatives open to her: If she is so much more competent in her profession than as a housekeeper that her earnings enable her to replace herself in the home with a first-class nurse, she could doubtless leave her children in the care of such a nurse after early infancy. But it is obviously poor economics for her, if she is truly a competent mother and housekeeper, to work outside the home if her earnings must all go to the nurse or housekeeper who understudies her in her own home!

The problem which each mother must decide for herself is, "At what age is it right that my children should be left to the care of others?" It is said that normal babies, after the difficult first months, may thrive better in the care of a competent children's nurse than in the hands of an emotional, inexperienced and incompetent mother. But because of this very emotional attitude, the normal woman is unwilling to yield her place to a hired nurse. It is this emotional pull of a mother to her infant that makes so hard the lot of the working-class mother, compelled by necessity to hand her tiny babe over to the care of the day-nurseries. Every woman desires to train her child according to her own ideals, and it is in plastic babyhood that strong impressions are made and when the child leans on the one person nearest him. Later on, when other companions, other teachers enter his life, his mother is another interesting individual who is part of the bigger group, but he no longer needs her so completely.

As long as she feels the pull and the need for her child, more overpowering than the call of her work, the business woman will prefer putting her energies into the home. But, she can take the second alternative, and even if she finds it impossible to obtain two or three hours of practical daily work in her profession or business, she can, nevertheless, keep in touch with it mentally. She may do no more than read trade papers, keep a file of clippings, attend lectures, drill daily, or read books relating to the business in which she is interested, but it keeps her abreast of the times, prevents her from becoming rusty, and prepared to resume work later on. Still, there are many women who continue a little of their work—perhaps selling insurance, real estate, and so forth—even tho they have a home and small children, and they sandwich their work in during the day quite conveniently.

Sometimes a question is raised as to the value of so perpetual a work-interest to women. After all, a large proportion, probably the majority of married women, can be supported somehow by their husbands, even when there are several small children. But there are reasons which none can afford to ignore. The first is this: that it is wrong and unsafe in principle for an adult to be economically helpless. A man who prevents his wife from exercising a marketable ability is in the same class of misguided husbands as the man who "shields" his wife from knowledge of his business difficulties—and so permits her to discover their penniless state at his funeral! That is hardly the time for her to begin to train for a paying occupation. There are few individuals in the world who are permanently protected against the possibility of being thrown on their own resources. Reverses due to loss of health, financial calamities, war or other casualties are likely to come into the life of any individual, and the best protection which any woman, married or unmarried, can have, is the training and equipment to support herself and her children, if need be.

Very often we are asked to commiserate with the poor tenement mother who must leave her infants and work outside for a living, and because she can only do unskilled factory work, or scrub floors or do a day's washing, she earns but $1 or $2 a day. But —the hardship is not that she must work outside the home. The real hardship is that she has not the training and the equipment to earn more than $1 or $2 per day. If she were more skilled, if she had improved in a premarital work interest or profession so that she had a higher industrial value, she might be able to replace herself in the home with a trained, dependable nurse or housekeeper, if the burden of supporting her little family fell on her shoulders.

There can be no question as to the soundness of the principle that an adult woman should be equipped for self-support. In the first place, the advantage of going to business with the definite purpose of making good and succeeding, even tho marriage is included in the program, can not fail to raise the achievements of the individual woman and the status of all women in business. In the second place, the woman with this purpose in mind builds for the future, so that she is equipped for permanent self-support. In the third place, when she has gone through the whole program, and reached the age when her children no longer need her care, is she not happier for possessing a definite interest of her own than is the woman to whom her children have been all in all, and whose interest in life may cease when her children no longer need her? And finally, there will be less fear and questioning of men's motives when women can stand independent, self-reliant, imposing no obligations on men and asking no favors.

All things considered, it must be admitted that the woman who shoulders three jobs—home, family and business—assumes a tremendous amount of work and responsibility. But where it is wisely managed it has developed women who are superior in every sense to those less ambitious. Mentally, physically, and ethically they are the stronger and more companionable women.

Chiefly, however, I hold that it is far better for two people to marry in early maturity, and both husband and wife to work, than to separate for economic reasons. Comparatively, there is no sacrifice in the difficult work of the married woman who manages her home and a business; nor does the young husband sacrifice much pride in consenting to her pursuing a business to help support their home. The great and unnecessary sacrifice is to give up the plan of life together because of the theory that the homemaker should not work.

On the other hand, supposing that, after spending considerable time on home-making as an avocation, the business woman doesn't marry, after all? Whether she marries or not, every business woman will be a happier woman if she has the preparation and the ambition for home-making. She should have a home of her own, even if she does not marry. Why should the unmarried business woman resign herself to the depressing isolation of a hired, characterless chamber, just because she hopes eventually "to marry and have a home of her own?" She will be far happier if she has a little home now, where she can cook and clean and sew and furnish and refurnish to her heart's content. One of the happiest of modern home-building tendencies is the growing custom of bringing into the home all sorts of amusements—like the phonograph or player-piano or even the home billiard table and so forth. Such things make people look forward to going home for play and comfort as they hitherto looked forward to going away from home for amusement. But too often, to the solitary business woman in her hall-bedroom, denying herself the material expressions of home that she would possess if she married, "home" is what a cynical wit once defined as "the place you stay in when there is nowhere else to go." And so, even if it does take extra effort, it is better for her to live now in the enjoyment of esthetic, even if simple, surroundings, which are expressions of her own personality, than to live in an atmosphere of ugly loneliness and sublime hope for the hereafter!

This, indeed, is the attitude of many modern business women. They desire more of a personal atmosphere than the rented room, or the average "woman's hotel," or the "working girl's home" can give them! There are hundreds of women who furnish a little home for themselves as soon as they can afford it. If they can not afford it, two or three girls live together, sharing the expenses and the tasks of the home. Certainly, there is more opportunity in this mode of living for developing homing instincts, which may atrophy when unused.

The great danger to the successful business woman is that, unless other instincts are cultivated, her business will overwhelm her personality, just as business overwhelms the "self-made" man sometimes. Some men have made the mistake of working exclusively at their business until they "get their little pile," in a belief that, after they had achieved wealth, they would rest and play —only to discover, eventually, that half a lifetime of work habits had crusht utterly the play instincts, or the ability to create other interests.

Many estimable business women have missed the joys of marriage and motherhood, but have so managed their lives that they have not been cheated entirely. They have been persistent in keeping themselves intellectually and emotionally well-rounded, and have made a home of their own in which they reared and educated adopted children. These women built life aggressively and fought for happiness, for, as Maréchal said of marriage, life, too, "is not a bed of roses, but a field of battle."

It is not dislike of work that keeps many business women pale and discontented; nor is it altogether loneliness. The cloud on the horizon of such a woman is that she is uncertain, and therefore pessimistic of the future. She hopes for marriage, but does not prepare for it. She lives in a state of pessimistic placidity, waiting for something nice to happen to her. And so she is not the "captain of her soul," but a human weather-vane, holding her peace of mind at the mercy of accidents and the caprices of her own moods. Her only salvation lies in learning how to live happily in the now, and planning her activities for life.

XI

THE FUTURE OF WOMEN IN BUSINESS

"THE whole education of women ought to be made relative to men. To please them, to be useful to them, to make themselves loved and honored by them, to educate them when young, to care for them when they are grown, to counsel them, to console them, and to make life agreeable and sweet to them—these are the duties of women at all times, and what should be taught them from infancy," wrote Rousseau over 150 years ago.[1]

Consequently, the Sophie for Rousseau's "Emile" was encouraged in art—but only with respect to the decoration of her person, so that she would be pleasing in the sight of her husband. "Why is it necessary for her to learn how to read and write at an early age?" he asks. "There are few who will not abuse, rather than use, this fatal science." She was taught to cipher a little because it would be needful to her in her

[1] Rousseau's "Emile."

household accounting. Her most important quality was to be docility, in order that she could obey man. Her mind was not to be profound. She was to accept all decisions from her father or her husband. This seems to have been adequate training for Sophie's career in eighteenth century matrimony, for at that time there was no other career open to her. As a matter of fact, she had an advantage over most modern women, because she was well trained for her ultimate job. When she achieved it, she was most capable in all its branches.

However, we may criticize the Rousseau ideal of education for women, we must admit that it contained one great advantage over modern methods for most women, in that Sophie knew what she was being educated for, and she concentrated on preparations for that goal. She knew that her destiny was "to please man and make life sweet to him," and she applied herself diligently to learning the arts that would help her accomplish her destiny.

The future of women in business will be affected by the exprest aim of their education. The future woman will be honest with herself, and will educate herself for work, or, like Rousseau's heroine, will recognize quite frankly that she prefers to concentrate on "the arts of pleasing men."

At present, these are observable facts about the average modern young woman. By her dress, by her manner, by her planless future as a self-sustaining individual, she fulfils beautifully a part of Rousseau's idea of woman. Her dominant interest in life is to attract and please men; she is interested in beauty only as it relates to the decorating of her person, and her mind is far from profound! But she does not begin to approach the Sophie of 150 years ago in intelligence and education for the practical responsibilities of marriage, and the making of a comfortable home. Rousseau's female heroine was ostensibly a fragile lily, wholly dependent on man. Actually, she was a most capable, sensible individual with a definite purpose, prepared to do her part in domestic life. The modern girl, by her sophistication, seems to be strong, self-reliant and independent but, actually, she requires more support from man than the old-fashioned woman, because she is not equipped nor educated to do a fair share in the business of matrimony.

"How can she be educated for marriage and home-making when she must earn her own living?" is asked indignantly. Can we assume, then, that her curriculum has been altered to fit the needs of the times? Is she now an expert in business instead of one in the home? Public opinion, observation and statistics indicate the contrary. Minimum wage commissions report that hundreds of thousands of women do not earn enough to keep body and soul together in decent comfort. Employers declare that many women do not earn the wages they are paid. It is possible that there is truth in this statement when you remember that two and one-half out of the eight million women employed in industries are under 20 years of age—and many of them have been at work since they were 10 years old. Indeed, 650,000 of these "women" are between the age of 10 and 15 years. How much marketable ability or education can a girl accumulate by the time she is 10 or 12 or 15 years old? Is she so strong mentally or physically that she can produce more than $1 a day in value?

The historian attributes her inadequacy to the degeneracy of the times, and disparagingly compares modern girls to our own colonial women who, between the ages of 12 and 20 produced the equivalent of more than $1 a day, altho this production was achieved within the home. They were expected to be wife, mother and manufacturer, and their reward was some of the food and clothing they produced. Most certainly these women were producers, but life was not kind to them, even in the best of families. In a study of records of 418 Yale husbands (1701-1745), William Hard[2] found that 147 lost their wives before they reached full middle age. We read how "first wife died at 24 leaving six children," and how "first wife died at 19 leaving three children." As Mr. Hard states: "The Colonial wife made an early start, but a quick finish. We are now in an age of delayed (or even omitted) marrying, and of a settled determination to keep on living!"

Now it is admitted that as far as home-making abilities are concerned most modern women are far behind the home-maker of

[2] "Women of To-morrow," by William Hard.

earlier days. Also, they are comparatively untrained for any other permanent work. When the typical young girl trains for business, it is casual training because she expects not to remain in business long. She doesn't even study home-making, because with the sublime hopefulness that flourishes in a democracy, she expects to marry above her own station in life. Subconsciously, she assumes that she will marry a man who can support her in luxury and provide her with servants, and so, of course, she does not need to train for housework herself.

But, regardless of the fact that lack of education, lack of ambition for work and consequent low pay, have resulted in a dilettante attitude of women toward business; regardless of the fact that the sincerest efforts of the average woman are directed to attracting men, object matrimony, women are in business to stay, and each year the number increases above the proportion of population increase. The number of women in business has increased 50 per cent. in 10 years, altho the number of men in business increased only 20 per cent. during the same period. In 1870 there were 9,982 women in clerical occupations alone; in 1910 there were 60 times as many —593,224 women.

But what can be done to make brighter the future of the woman in business, and who will remain in business whether she faces this fact early or not. What can be done to improve the status of the underpaid, unhappy "working girl?" "Minimum wage" is only a partial remedy which attacks the result, not the cause, of unpreparedness. Minimum wage does not equip a girl for a better job. Forcing employers to pay $8 instead of $6 makes it possible for a girl who has the job to live in decent physical comfort, but does it provide an $8 job for every girl, and as long as she wants to hold it? What is the future of the girl who stays on contentedly in her $8 job, does not marry, and at the age of 30 loses it?

If we must have legislation, let it be constructive and anticipatory as well as remedial. The state has a duty to the adult woman who is so inefficient that she can not command a living wage.

Any woman over 18 years old who is not

able to earn more than $8 per week without a minimum wage law, ought to be sent back to school and trained at public expense until she is equipped for more than an $8 job. It is not her fault, nor her disgrace that she can not earn more, but the fault of inadequate educational laws, and her own insufficient means to get a fair start in life. Just as needful as compulsory education for children is the need of provision by the state for the compulsory training of women who are not worth more than $8 a week Adequate training will not only make her more efficient, but she will be dissatisfied even with the generous minimum wage established by law, and she will be ambitious enough to plan for progress.

The woman who has entered an industry at an early age has suffered from two handicaps which can be eliminated only by education. One is the lack of adequate preparation for making her self-supporting on a good wage. The second is that she does not know how to get joy out of living. But supposing the woman of the future commands an adequate wage. Will her sublime efficiency be concentrated on work? Will she be completely happy when she is well paid? That is only half the program.

The saddest aspect in the condition of the much-investigated "working girl" is not only that she is ill paid, but that she does not know how to live. She has not been educated in esthetic and spiritual interests which would enable her to make beautiful her surroundings and to draw on that inner source of happiness, capacity for thinking. She depends for happiness on the stimulation of cheap, outer, ephemeral things, because they are all she knows If we had an adequate educational system which taught girls how to live as well as how to work, there would be fewer of the tragedies suffered by girls who consider amusements and fine clothes an excellent exchange for morality. It is not inherent wickedness nor temporary thoughtlessness, but fundamental ignorance concerning the real basis of happiness; and that is what education is for, to provide a basis for selecting values, and to teach us how to live.

"Civilization," says Lester F. Ward,[3] "is a process of lengthening youth." Savage

[3] "Pure Sociology," by Lester F. Ward.

peoples mature early, but they also fade early. A girl on the African Gold Coast is married at 13, but she is a wrinkled old woman at 30. In the United States we find that illiteracy, child labor and immature marriages go hand in hand. Wherever the responsibilities of maturity are thrust on childhood, we find that the vicious circle of illiteracy, child labor and immature marriages repeats itself endlessly. Compare the standing of various states according to the following table compiled from the 1910 Census:

PER CENT. IN EACH GROUP OF STATES

	Illiterate women over 10 years of age	*Girls at work 10 to 13 years of age*	*Girls married between 15 and 19 years of age*
	Per Cent.	*Per Cent.*	*Per Cent.*
New England States...	5.2	.4	6.
Middle Atlantic........	5.7	.8	6.9
East North Central.....	3.3	.6	8.4
West North Central.....	2.9	1.1	9.2
South Atlantic	16.1	20.1	15.2
East South Central....	17.3	22.8	18.5
West South Central...	13.8	18.1	18.9
Mountain	7.5	1.3	13.2
Pacific	2.5	.5	9.6

It is undeniable that if the business women of the future are to be intelligent and contented, the first step in preparedness is to make certain that they will have a "lengthened youth." It is our civic duty to enforce laws to overcome those conditions which make tired, joyless adults out of children. On account of high specialization to-day, it is endurance as much as skill that is needed in industry. A girl under 18 years of age has not had time to develop the physical endurance she will need if she is to remain in an industry many years, especially if most of the years of early adolescence have been spent in exhausting labor. And so a preparedness program for the business woman of the future would make her, figuratively speaking, a ward of the state until her 18th year. In other words, the compulsory education law would be advanced from the 14-year limit (as it is in New York, or 16 years as it is in an enlightened state like Ohio) to the 18-year limit. There would be no breaking-off point between the elementary and the high school at the age of 14 to give the child time to ask whether she should continue to study, or plunge head foremost into wage-earning. The school for the average girl's training would be a "one-piece" school which she entered at the age of six or seven and where she completed work at the age of 18 or 19. The average college girl of to-day completes her studies at the age of about 22, and because she has been helped and financed through a long educational period she usually earns twice or three times[4] as much as the working girl of the same age who lacks adequate training for work and for life.

If a girl's parents or guardians have not the means to support her through a 12-year educational period, it would be far less costly for the state to finance her than, several years later, for the state to pay commissions "to investigate the causes of immorality among working girls"; or to have to support hospitals because she can not earn enough to pay her way in time of sickness; or to have to pay mothers' pensions to her because she has no training for work which will enable her to support her children. In this country we support

[4] "Commercial Work and Training for Girls," Eaton & Stevens. "Public Schools and Women in Office Service."

many institutions for the alleviation of conditions. Would it not be somewhat far-sighted to spend more on preventives of such conditions and on educational institutions so that every girl at maturity should be equipped for self-support, educated to do good work, and possest of a spiritual basis for a happy and self-respecting life?

Under the prevalent school system, children give no thought to their ultimate occupation. There are a few exceptions, as under the Gary plan, and a few other plans operated in several cities; but in the majority of schools at present, there is no definite provision for the training of the child for its occupation. Our juvenile educational system keeps children in a state of spongelike receptivity to knowledge which is unrelated to the problems of real life. Suddenly, with little warning and no preparation, they are called upon to make the important decision as to a practical occupation in which they may earn a livelihood.

Is the following a too-ambitious program for the business woman of the future? She will have twelve years in which to select her ultimate occupation—from the age of 6 to

18. Her daily studies will be so arranged that, as Prof. John Dewey[5] points out, she will "form the habit of connecting the limited information acquired with the activities of life. The primary and fundamental problem," he says, "is not to prepare individuals to work at particular callings, but to be vitally and sincerely interested in the calling upon which they must enter if they are not to be social parasites, and to be informed as to the social and scientific bearings of that calling. The aim is not to prepare breadwinners. But since men and women are normally engaged in bread-winning vocations they need to be intelligent in the conduct of households, the care of children, the management of farms and shops, and in the political conduct of a democracy where industry is a prime factor."[5]

To this end the education of the future business woman will combine theoretical learning with practical training. The work of the Gary schools may be used as a model by which to educate the women of the future. Here girls, as well as boys, get training in cooking, sewing, printing, carpen-

[5] "Schools of To-morrow," by John and Evelyn Dewey.

tering, painting, bookkeeping and many other branches of business as well as academic education. They are given opportunity to use all their faculties. They are taught how to use their hands as well as their minds, and all class-work is related to real needs. They learn botany through actual gardening, chemistry through food preparation, and all pupils receive a course in the elements of science, so that they have a rational grasp of principles. Here is interesting proof that such all-round education as the Gary plan affords is not more costly than the less complete curricula of other types of schools.

A comparison of per capita cost of schools in Gary and New York [6]:

	Gary	*New York*
Per capita cost, including instructions and educational supplies	$31.72	$ 40.24
High school	....	104.74
Per capita cost in schools which include kindergarten, elementary, vocational shops and high school:		
Boys	56.12	86.48
Girls	32.85	142.32

In New York, Cincinnati, Philadelphia and many other cities the "continuation" school,

[6] Alice B. Fernandez, in New York *Tribune*, April 25, 1915.

where girls and boys already in an industry may divide their time between school studies and their work in shop or factory, has been tried already with good results.

Perhaps the women's colleges of the future will render service to students and to business by preparing students adequately for business careers; that is, by including in the curriculum some studies which will enable the pupil to relate her knowledge to business needs. At present, too many college women consider only teaching, or literary, or sociological work as occupations worthy of their training. But young men go to colleges like Yale or Harvard as a preparation for a business career. Why should not women do likewise? That there exists demand for such training among women is indicated by the fact that some of the men's colleges where there are schools of business administration (as Harvard, Columbia and New York University) are throwing open these courses to women also.

At present, many college women declare that it does not pay them to take a $5,000 education in order to get a $12-a-week job. That, however, is what men are willing to do. They begin at the very bottom of the ladder, just as the uneducated worker does. Stepping from the Harvard campus into overalls in a factory is common among typical, red-blooded American young men, and it has been the subject of many of our most popular romances read by our most refined young college women. These young men earn no more than other factory operatives at the time they start, because they are not worth more in the beginning occupation.

But in New York City an employment organization for college women refused to place any registrees in any position paying less than $15 a week at the start. Many college women refuse to start at a low-paid beginning occupation, failing to realize that their value to industry at the beginning is small—just as a young college man's value is small. But in a few years the college-bred man can outstrip the uneducated worker both in salary and responsibility.

There is another factor to consider. At present many employers are literally compelled to install in their own plants schools and courses either to supplement the deficient education of employees or to supply the technical education needed for the business. It is a purely mathematical proposition that, when employers are relieved of the expense of educating employees, they can afford to pay more in salaries. This will make business a more profitable field for the woman with an expensive education, but she will have to take the initiative and first prove her worth.

Out of a sound basis of education will arise love and respect for work, and so the business woman of the future will not only do her own job well, but she will possess a keen mental curiosity about all business. She will be an omnivorous reader of information which affects her business progress. Like ambitious young men, she, too, will take business courses; she will study finance and the principles of business administration; she will keep up-to-date on legislation affecting business. She will read business books and trade papers to keep abreast of conditions in her own industry and in the large field of commerce. She will do her part in commercial clubs and be interested in civic movements for the development of local prosperity. In appreciation of the pioneering work done for her by former generations of business women, she will recognize her responsibility to all women who work. She will help in public movements to raise the status of women at work. Individually she will do her share by maintaining the principle of "good pay for good work," and by refusing to work for a lower wage than the standard simply because she is a woman, or because she is one of the few women who does not need the money.

To sum up the program of the business woman of the future: First, she will have a broad basis of education, so that she knows how to live intelligently. Second, she will be definitely educated for a definite work. She will have an insatiable thirst for business information, and her interest will extend to principles beyond the routine of her immediate tasks. Third, she will have a large goal, because she will have aspirations for a complete business career, the career that culminates in a high executive post. Fourth, she will have a home of her own, whether or not she marries, because she will do all she can to attain a complete and happy womanhood.

To do her share in the new business the future woman will be trained to think, and not alone to obey orders. Unlike the Rousseau woman who was trained for a dependent existence, she will have a mind sharpened by years of thinking, and made profound through training in the principles of science and philosophy. The woman's view-point is even to-day of especial value in business. With a better grasp of business principles, the woman of the future will know how to make the most of her asset and to give her individual contribution to the advance of business. She will plan to have a business of her own, and she will equip herself for executive responsibility early in her career. It is true that the ten or fifteen million women in our population who will be self-supporting can not all be executives. But ambition and the self-discipline for executive work will make them better workers wherever they are.

The business woman of the future will plan her life independently. Marriage will be part of her plan, just as it is part of the plan of the normal man. When it comes she will be prepared for the duties of home management, and content if it is necessary for her to relinquish her career for some years because her mind has been prepared for that contingency, and she knows how to keep in touch with her business during years of absence from active work. But she will never "have to marry for a meal ticket," as one woman put it. She will marry only for the highest instincts. If she does not marry, she will know how to make life complete and happy, nevertheless, because she will know how to select the real values of life. She will know what is really beautiful, because she has been educated in this knowledge, and her esthetic ideas will not be limited to the adornment of her own person, but will be used to beautify her surroundings, wherever she happens to be. She will know how to be useful also in a civic and social sense, and her enjoyment of life will extend to deeper things than ephemeral amusements.

The business woman of the future will be complete and radiant womanhood—strong, self-sustaining and full of the joy of living.

PART II

Occupational

PREFACE

I HAVE not sought in the following pages to set forth the complete and specific steps to be taken in the pursuit of any one occupation. It would be presumptuous and futile to endeavor to encompass within the space of a single chapter information about business that requires months or years of study in order to achieve proficiency. There are excellent specialized schools and books to teach these subjects. The names of many of them are given in the bibliography at the end of the book.

My endeavor has been to indicate present requirements and tendencies in business occupations, so as to provide a basis on which to adjust oneself to the business in which one is interested. The word "business" is used in the sense of "commerce"—the interchange of merchandise or property. Consequently, business occupations are here interpreted as the work of selling and buying, and the executive, creative and detail work which accompanies the business of selling and buying. It is true there are other occupations which sooner or later will fall under the classification of business. We are told that agriculture is a profitable business; the work of the home is being specialized and put on a business basis, and many of the professions are being operated very much more like a merchandising business. There is opportunity for woman in all of these fields, but a discussion of all such work is not within the province of this book. We are considering here only the methods by which the foundation of a typical business career in the United States—buying, selling and its accompaniments—can be laid.

The information which follows is to encourage business women to interest themselves in more than one occupation. There are several reasons for this. I know we are "living in an age of specialization," but it is also true that industry changes so much that the one job on which you have specialized may disappear to-morrow because of some new business invention or development. And so I believe that every woman should have more than one occupation, so that she can fall back on the second if the first fails her.

The problem of export is one worthy of much careful attention by the business woman who plans ahead. Within the next decade the export developments are destined to change considerably American industry. Consequently, there is need for business women to begin early to familiarize themselves with foreign customs and languages and trade developments, for export will be a vast American industry after the great conflict is over. I have not devoted space to the important subject of export. Authoritative books are gradually growing in number, and the titles of some good publications are given in the bibliography.

One of the objections often made to certain systems of vocational guidance is that their conclusions are based on a too-limited view of an occupation *per se,* instead of a study of an occupation as it relates to the whole commercial system. If every office woman, no matter how humble her job, would make it her business to know office work in all its branches; if every saleswoman would educate herself in mental grasp of the entire field of selling; if every woman who entered business would vision business as a whole, studying it from every possible angle, would it not be much easier for women to adjust themselves to changing conditions in business? Would they not have less reason to dread the possible "shake-up" that might deprive them of a particular little job?

The woman who has so much information about many sides of business is able to make adjustments in her career whenever business vicissitudes require, and she is comparatively safe from the horror of "joblessness." Adaptability to business requirements is far more important than any intensified proficiency in one tiny job—a proficiency that has been attained because larger elements have been sacrificed. You may lose your little job, but if you have knowledge and aptitude about business as a whole you need not worry. You will find a new niche.

A WELL-PLANNED OFFICE
Note flat-top desks with few drawers, convenient file arrangement, and indirect lighting system.

XII

THE OFFICE FIELD FOR WOMEN

"OVERCROWDED!" That is the perpetual criticism leveled at office work. In 1910 there were nearly 600,000 women in clerical work (one-third as many as men). It was reported that 541 schools teaching commercial subjects had an attendance of 134,778 (72,887 men and 61,891 women). Now, if each year's influx of workers into an office consisted of "trained" workers, we in the United States would be in the sad position of Germany before the war, where every man was educated far beyond his job, and the clerk who wrapt your package was, likely as not, a master of four languages and half a dozen sciences.

Admittedly, office work, taken as a whole, is usually overcrowded and underpaid, but that is only because the office has been poorly served. A large proportion of office workers are grammar-school girls (some of them not even graduates) who have been railroaded through a rapid, so-called "business school" and then foisted on a luckless business office. Inefficient workers in large numbers have dragged down the wage standards of the field as a whole until now it is only the worker who has recognizable ability, plus the ability to sell her services well, who is really paid the sum that intelligently performed office work is worth. This does not mean that there is no opportunity in office work for the ambitious woman. On the contrary, the very fact that offices are besieged by inefficient and indifferent workers makes the woman of training and ambition all the more welcome

Here is the strong attraction of office work for the ambitious woman. Put a trained, intelligent, ambitious woman in any kind of office job—the lowest there is—and she is in a position leading to executive work, because all the executive work of an organization emanates from the office. The policies concerning manufacturing, sales, credits and all departments are not determined in the factory or by salesmen on the road, but by executives in the office. The office is the clearing-house of information for the entire business. It is the coign of vantage from which a bird's-eye view of the whole business is obtained. On the following chart are shown the various office jobs and the advancement to which they lead:

CLERICAL GROUP
- Addressing
- Circularizing and mailing
- Copying
- Filing
- Entry work—order and billing
- Stenography and typing
- Bookkeeping and calculating

Leading to

POSTS REQUIRING INITIATIVE
- Private secretary
- Correspondent
- Selling representative
- Statistician
- Cashier
- Purchasing agent

Leading to

EXECUTIVE GROUP
- Manager of a department:
  - Advertising
  - Branch store
  - Collection
  - Credit and adjustment
  - Office
  - Sales
  - Traffic
  - Etc.

Leading to

ADMINISTRATIVE GROUP	General manager President Vice-president Secretary Member board of directors

"Clerical work" at one time meant "general office work," or doing a little bit of everything. The "office girl" addrest envelops, answered the telephone, made out the bills, typed circulars, and between times ran on errands, for performing all of which functions she was usually paid less than any one else in the office, because she was untrained for any definite work and received her business education in the office she served. In larger organizations, however, there is no such thing as "general office work." Each branch is specialized, and to a large extent office machinery has superseded human labor.

Here is one of the developments of the office that has affected the woman office worker considerably, and in many cases in a most favorable way: For example, a young girl who spent several months learning how to typewrite earned about $1 a day addressing envelops as soon as she became proficient enough to hold such a position. The work was monotonous and certainly as hard manual labor as she would have done in any factory. Then came the addressing machine. Now, if she can operate an addressing machine, make the stencils, etc., she can turn out many times as much work as she did before, and can earn twice as much, also the work is somewhat less monotonous. Following is a comparison of office workers' salaries with and without machines, based on estimates from five large cities:

AVERAGE WAGES PAID FOR "GENERAL OFFICE WORK"

	Per Week
Entry or bill clerk	$10
Filing clerk, untrained	8
Copyist	7
Mailing, folding, clerk	6
Bookkeeper (woman)	15
Cashier (woman)	12
Typist	8

AVERAGE WAGES PAID OPERATORS OF MODERN MACHINES OR METHODS

	Per Week
Trained file clerk	$14
Adding machine operator	10
Billing machine operator	15
Comptometer operator	12
Mimeograph operator	10
Multigraph operator	15
Phonograph operator	14

It is a curious fact that, while young girls spend money without hesitation on some attractive "business course" that sends them off in the same old rut half equipped, few take pains to learn how to operate the machines found in the modern office, in spite of the fact that such knowledge would increase their salaries. Very few schools teach the use of all business machines, but the information is readily available from the manufacturers, who are always glad to teach any one to operate their devices. In fact, one manufacturer of an addressing machine offered to pay $12 a week to an intelligent girl if she would learn how to operate his machine and then teach it to clerks in buyers' offices. And at a time when stenographers were a drug on the market, and were glad to get $8-a-week-jobs, he could not get the right kind of help, because the stenographers "were afraid to lose speed" by doing other than stenographic work. The fact that in this new work they might find a bigger opportunity than in some stenographic post escaped them utterly.

There are many advantages open to the woman who learns how to use the most up-to-date devices, and who makes it her business to know the difference between various competitive makes. She not only makes herself more desired than the girl with only average equipment, but she puts herself in the way of a higher job—that of purchasing agent for the office. Men are constantly amazed at the ignorance and awkwardness of office women with tools—the very tools they use. The average typist, even after many years of experience, is unable to make the simplest repairs to her machine. The office boy knows more about the mechanism of her typewriter than she does. Of course, the underlying reason is the difference in the education of boys and girls, and the peculiar superstition instilled into the latter that it is unladylike for a woman to know how to handle a hammer, a plane or a saw. Nevertheless, she can always learn. It may not be possible for her to know everything about the office machines listed here, but she can at least keep herself informed about those which might possibly be valuable in her office in the saving of time and labor.

MACHINERY USED IN MODERN OFFICES

Addressing, Mailing and Duplicating Machines

Addressograph
Elliott addressing machine
Montague addressing machine
Rapid addressing machine
Multigraph duplicating
Planotype duplicating
Writerpress
Mimeograph (stencil)
Library Bureau letter-copying machine
Mail-ometer envelop sealer
Thexton envelop sealer
Simplex envelop sealer
Simmons envelop opener
O. K. envelop opener
Cummins postage stamp perforator
Fixo postage stamp affixer
Multipost postage stamp affixer
Signagraph signature machine
Diograph stencil cutting machine
Neostyle (stencil)
Schapirograph (gelatine roll type)
Daus (gelatine roll type)
Billograph (gelatine roll type)
Plex (Clay type)

Addressing, Mailing and Duplicating Machines

Expert (Clay type)
Eureka (Clay type)
Express (Clay type)
Roneo letter copying machine
Peerless envelop moistener
Bushnell strap package fastener
Ever-Ready gummed tape fastener
Lightning envelop opener
Wing-Horton mailing machines
Standard stamp affixer
Simplex stamp affixer
America canceling machine
Scriptograph signature machine
Bradley stencil cutting machine

Computing and Billing Machines

Burroughs adding machine
Wales adding machine
Barrett adding machine
Dalton adding machine
Comptometer adding machine
Moon-Hopkins adding machine
Ellis adding machine
Remington-Wahl adding typewriter (for billing)
National cash register
Standard computing scales
Stimpson computing scales
Hollerith tabulating machine
Elliott-Fisher adding type (billing)
Underwood adding type
Monarch billing machine
Acme billing machine
Millionaire calculating machine
T. I. M. calculating machine
Ensign electric calculating machine
X & X calculating machine
National computing scales
Veeder counting machine
Bates numbering machine

Writing, Filing and Indexing: Machines and Systems

Shouperior Autographic registers
Invincible autographic registers
Photostat (photographing records)
Rectograph (photographing records)
Cyclometer (for measuring typewriting)
Edison dictating machine
Dictaphone dictating machine
Remington typewriter
Underwood typewriter
Royal typewriter
Victor typewriter
Monarch typewriter
New Century typewriter
Noiseless typewriter

Art metal steel file cases
Safe-cabinet metal filing case
Ever-last metal filing case
Globe-Wernicke metal filing cases
Rand instantaneous indexing system
Smith's adjustable indexing tabs
Graef signal indexing tabs
Y. & E. everlasting indexing tabs
K. & E. blue-printing machines
Buckeye blue-printing machines
Defiance check-writer
Protectograph check protector
Munson cushion keys for typewriter
Stenotype (shorthand machine)
Anderson (shorthand machine)
L. C. Smith typewriter
Oliver typewriter
Sun typewriter
Smith-Premier typewriter
Hammond typewriter
Yost typewriter
Smead bandless file envelop
Bushnell bandless file envelop
Smith card index pointers
Vise card index pointers
Iliff map and tack system
Multiplex map and tack system
Rand-McNally system

Intercommunicating Systems

Telautograph (reproducing handwriting between distant points)
Auto-cable (signal bells)
Lamson carriers
Dictograph (magnifying reproduction of voice at a distance)
Western Electric interior telephone

Miscellaneous Office Devices and Systems

Jupiter pencil sharpeners
Planetary pencil sharpeners
Boston pencil sharpeners
Phelps time locks
Calculagraph time record
International time register
Stromberg time register
Comptocard (to record time spent in office operations)
F. & T. coupon cutters
Cummins coupon cutters
American combination bracket book-holder
Extension directory and book-holder
Emerald desk lights
Almond-flexo desk lamp
American copy press
Standard copy press
Little Giant copy tank
Automatic time stamp
Commercial utilities time stamp
Perry time stamp
Duff wage tables
Johnson coin-packaging machine
Batdorf coin-packaging machine
Numbering machines
Clipless paper fasteners

The girl who makes it her business to know many modern machines prepares herself for better opportunities than if she had ignored such information, for these reasons:

First—She can help in the wise selection of labor-saving devices for the office, preventing useless expense, because she knows the difference between various machines and knows which are unsuitable. If she continues to show herself well posted and a shrewd buyer she may in time be promoted to the post of "purchasing agent." Usually this is a man's job; but there are women holding such positions who have created them for themselves simply by knowing thoroughly the office-equipment field, cost of machines and points about competitive makes, cost of paper, printing, etc

Second—She will know how to prevent waste. It has been estimated that the cost of writing letters varies between a minimum of 6½ cents to 41 cents per letter, the average cost being 14 cents per letter. The girl who is alert enough to study labor-saving machines and methods, and can suggest ways to cut down the cost of letters in her own office distinguishes herself immediately, and is in line for promotion over those with less energy and initiative.

Third—The stenographer or clerk who can say, in a letter of application, that she can operate an addressing machine, or an adding machine, or a billing machine, naturally receives the preference over those applicants without this information

Fourth—The more the office woman knows about many modern machines, the more intelligently will she be able to operate her own machine. She will know how to keep it in good running condition and to make many simple repairs herself

Knowledge of machines is simply one more asset to the office woman's business capital. She should also have the habit of using all labor-saving equipment. Many business men complain that they spend money having labor-saving machines or attachments installed, but that the office workers—men just as much as women—do not use them. Why buy time-savers or labor-savers? It is the office worker's business to use every possible method or device that saves, if the investment is to yield a profit.

Machinery has done away with much of

the old-time methods of clerking. The mathematical brain of the bookkeeper is not so highly prized since automatic bookkeeping and calculating machines have entered the office. The best bill clerk is not necessarily a lightning calculator as of yore, but may be a good operator of the billing machine. Parallel with the advent of machinery that eliminates the drudgery of computation in business there has grown up a greater demand for statistics about business and a higher appreciation of their value. In many large organizations there is a permanent statistician employed, or the services of an outside statistician are called into requisition. His duty is to assemble data and figures, prepare charts and analyses which summarize conditions in parts of the business, or in an industry. The statistician is comparatively new in business, altho the government has always employed numbers of statisticians in many departments, and women among them. There are very few women statisticians in business—possibly for the same reason that there are few women accountants.

The "certified public accountant" is another profession which has developed from the growing demand of business for more statistical facts. Keeping his books nicely balanced is the end and aim of the bookkeeper. But the accountant is the glorified bookkeeper, and the keeping of books is the basis of his work, not the goal, because the high-type public accountant is really a business analyst and counsel.

There are differing opinions regarding opportunities for women in accounting work. There is the ever-popular theory that women can do anything that men do, and that there is no insurmountable barrier to them in accounting work, and this is perfectly tenable. But it is necessary to face the fact that accounting, like law, architecture and a few other professions, is an occupation in which women meet with prejudice. It is not logical opposition which can be overcome with comparative ease, but blind prejudice that refuses even to consider woman's possible abilities. The explanation offered is this. The business man calls in the accountant to examine books, straighten out tangles and make recommendations for improvement. He looks up to the accountant for superior advice in the management or reconstruction of his affairs. Naturally, therefore, he prefers an accountant with a broad experience and sound business judgment. He is prejudiced against the young, inexperienced accountant, and more or less against the woman accountant. The average business man will not readily admit to a woman that she can know more about his affairs than he does, nor is he inclined to yield to her counsels.

Nevertheless, this is the same kind of prejudice that women have always had to contend with, and with which women lawyers, women doctors, and women architects still grapple. And in spite of the prejudice, many women in these occupations have forged ahead much further than their masculine contemporaries. It is inevitable that eventually all prejudice against women in such advanced occupations will melt away. When the attitude of women toward their work changes, the attitude of men toward women in high business positons will change.

In the meantime, women of ambition and ability will have the courage to do pioneer work when necessary. Why should the ambitious business woman stay content in a bookkeeping job when she has the brains, experience and desire to do higher accounting? The best schools of accounting open their doors to women as well as to men. When she graduates she will probably have to be content to work for some other accountant instead of launching at once into a business of her own. But thousands of young men accountants must do the same thing. Very few indeed can begin at once with a clientele. It takes years to establish a reputation which attracts clients, and these years must be spent in gathering experience. The woman who is serious-purposed, and determined to succeed, will be willing to work hard, prepare well and battle with obstacles—just as men do; and she, too, will achieve the high place that men reach.

Filing is probably the only office job that can not be checked up. The stenographer can see her errors; the bookkeeper can "balance" his records, but the filing clerk who happened to misplace Lawson's letter in Dawson's file goes on her way in blissful ignorance of her error, until the unlucky day when Lawson's letter is desired and can not be found. Filing, by its very nature, offers more opportunities for error per unit of work than any other job. And yet, the file clerk usually is the girl who has not had an opportunity for a business education, and fell into filing because it was the only office job in which training was not demanded. The other girls would "show her how."

But because of the growing need of available facts, and the larger variety and amount of records that are preserved in the average business, a need has arisen for the trained file clerk. The old-fashioned file clerk stayed in her rut and was content with $8 or $9 per week. The trained file clerk now earns from $10 to $20 per week, and even more, and she is a good investment at the price because she works more rapidly, her percentage of error is smaller, and she has an equipment that makes her a producer.

The modern file clerk, especially if she is a woman of education and previous business experience, is a first-aid-to-business. She enters the office, and after several days of study of its needs, can formulate a filing system that fits the peculiarities of the business. Moreover, with an eye to the best interests of business, she is able to suggest more extensive use of the information contained in the files, just as the public librarian can suggest means of getting value out of the city's literary storehouse. That type of filing specialist is finding no difficulty in getting jobs that pay $20 a week and more, and her work keeps her in touch with so many phases of business that it is a constant education to her on her road upward. She doesn't necessarily stick to one job for years. Sometimes she is a specialist; she is a "consulting filing expert," spending only two or three months, or even less, in each office, installing a good system, and training girls to operate the system correctly.

There are now special schools of filing in New York and other large cities where filing, as a complete subject, is taught. There are many standard filing methods such as the Dewey Decimal, the Williams Railroad Classification, Alphabetic, Alphabetic-numeric, Subject, Direct in conjunction with index, Geographic, and other methods. Then there are special systems of filing for almost every business, *i.e.*, Banking, Brokers, Contracts, Corporations, Engineering, Institutions and Associations Insurance, Law, Mail order, Publishers, Real Estate, and Sales. Card-indexing, and follow-up methods are depended upon largely in the conduct of mail-order business and other species of advertising, and neglect or inaccuracy is costly. Consider the following statistics on the cost of filing government communications (prepared by the Bureau of Efficiency and Economy at Washington), and compare them with the cost of filing in your own office, and perhaps you will see how the cost of filing can be reduced as well as the actual work made more efficient by trained file clerks.

COST OF FILING GOVERNMENT COMMUNICATIONS

Department	*Per 1,000*	*cents each*
Post Office	$ 6.53	or ½
Agricultural	6.96	½
Treasury	8.24	4/5
Navy	12.87	1
Commerce and Labor	12.89	1
State	13.08	1
War	16.18	1½
Justice	18.33	1 4/5
Interior	20.33	2

Filing has been called a "blind alley" job, but only because it has been in the category of "unskilled" labor. It presents many opportunities to the trained woman of intelligence, both in good compensation and in means for improving a much-neglected work.

Stenography is admittedly the occupation that brings the worker closest to an opportunity for executive education. Concentrated information about a business passes through the stenographer's book. She is the bridge between the business and the public. And yet we find that stenography is distinguished mainly by the pitiful inefficiency of the average worker. The fault is not hers, either. It is due to an inadequate educational system that permits a girl to "graduate" from elementary schools with scarcely more than a bowing acquaintance with the three R's. It is due also to lack of proper educational supervision, which makes it possible for fly-by-night "business schools" to claim to give a good business course, including stenography and typewriting in six months. Indeed, some of them offer to do the trick in thirty days.

In an investigation made among employers and employment agencies, the opinion was obtained that the reason for so much unemployment among women stenographers is not that the field is overcrowded—there never was a time when an intelligent stenographer could not be placed in a good position within a reasonable period, unless her personality was objectionable. The real reason is that most girls who call themselves stenographers are ill-prepared, uneducated, and a hindrance to business men instead of a help. It is lack of preparation, or unpleasant habits, or an unattractive personality, that keep the stenographer out of a job.

How can a woman with stenographic aspirations prepare for a good post? A suggestion may be culled from the following experiences: Two young girls who had been lifelong friends graduated from an elementary school together. They were both intelligent and fairly ambitious, but they came of poor parents and neither could afford the college education they would have liked. So they entered different offices, doing some kind of clerical work at which they earned a small wage. Then Mary decided she wanted to be a stenographer. She resigned her job, looked up the "business school" which guaranteed to teach stenography quicker than any other school in town, and, at the end of sixty days to throw in a job into the bargain! Mary was intelligent and conscientious, and when she obtained her first job at stenography (at $6 per week) she stuck to it and worked hard. Unlike many other lightning-trained stenographers, she was not a "drifter." She held on to her job as tightly as she could, and at the end of six years she was still the stenographer—earning $12 per week and entirely satisfied.

Jane happened to be of a more ambitious type. When she decided that stenography was better than office work, she asked also, "What is better than stenography?" She saw that the fair stenographers in the office were earning $12 or $15 a week after many years of experience, and that did not seem a big enough goal to her. So after she had spent some weeks studying stenography in an evening school, and found progress slow, she determined on a new course of preparation. She resigned her job and borrowed money to finance herself through a four-year commercial course in high school. She earned $10 a week in her first position after graduation, and in three years mounted to $25 per week as stenographer and "right hand" of the president of the company.

There is nothing marvelous in the difference of achievement between these girls. The first had nothing to offer except her bare mechanical skill as a stenographer and typist. Even after her "business course" in stenography she was still superbly ignorant of the principles of business and had to learn much in her first post before she could be useful. But the second girl had a desirable group of assets to any business. She had sound theoretical business training. She knew something of business principles. She had been educated to think and to concentrate.

Even from the standpoint of dollars and cents value alone, it is more profitable to borrow money for a good preparatory education for business than to attempt economy by rushing through a cheap, quick business course. It is true that it will take a few years of work to repay the loan, and it is likely also that the girl with a high school or college education may have to start at as low a salary as the girl without this training. But, the girl with education forges ahead far more rapidly in compensation and responsibility—not to speak of the greater mental satisfactions she gets out of work and out of life because of her secondary education.

There is opportunity for excellent earnings in the stenographic field, as is shown by the following table of wages which is a composite average wage prevailing in a group of large cities: Minimum for beginners, $5 to $8 per week; average salary paid, $12 per week; maximum salary paid, $25 per week. There are exceptions to this maximum. Expert law stenographers frequently earn up to $50 per week; while official court reporters (and there are women engaged in this branch, particularly in the West) earn from $1,000 to $6,000 per year. Public stenographers who succeed in a business of their own earn anywhere from $2,000 to $5,000 per year, and some earn as high as $10,000. The two immediate superior jobs to the stenographer are (1) a business of her own—that is, a public stenographic office; (2) a "private secretaryship."

As the greater part of public stenographic work is done on credit, the woman who opens her own office should have a balance of at least $250 in bank after buying her office supplies, typewriting machine, and paying her rent. This amount will see her through until her first month's bills are paid, unless she happens to strike an unusually deprest business time. Women who have prospered claim that the public stenographer must be not only a good stenographer but a good saleswoman and business manager. She must know how to obtain business, and how to keep expenses down, and then she is able to make a good profit—possibly between 20 and 25 per cent. But the earnings are likely to vary largely from week to week—next to nothing some weeks, and in other weeks running into hundreds of dollars. Therefore, she operates on a basis of yearly, not weekly earnings—not feeling unduly jubilant the week she pockets $200 and deprest and hopeless the following week when her sales record shows only $20 earned. The work is likely to have its dull seasons just like many trades, and they must be anticipated.

The successful public stenographer is equipped with some specialized knowledge (unless she is in a hotel or residential section when only ordinary material will be dictated to her). For example, if she is in the financial district, it is best for her to know financial and law forms and technical phrases. If she is in the exporting section of the business district, she must either have a knowledge of several languages, or be in touch with a translator, and possibly should employ one on her staff as soon as business justifies.

The success of the public stenographer depends on her business ability and personality. She must be a good saleswoman, able to build a large clientele. She must be painfully prompt; once she disappoints a client she is likely to lose him forever. Unlike the stenographer in an office who has to grow accustomed to the idiosyncrasies of the one or two men she works for, the public stenographer has to work for dozens or hundreds of people She must, therefore, drill herself to be exceedingly tactful, agreeable and adaptable, with an unlimited fund of good humor and patience.

"Private secretary" is the title which every stenographer covets. Business men know this so well that it has become a joke, and one merchant, more shrewd than generous, instead of giving his stenographer an increase in salary which she asked for, told her that she was promoted to the title of "private secretary." She then could sign some letters "private secretary," and was content. What is a "secretary," and how shall a stenographer know whether she is a secretary? The word "secretary" is derived from the classical Latin "secretus," meaning secret; hence a confidential officer or attendant. In medieval ages the "secretary" was a notary, scribe, treasurer, or sexton; and it also meant a council chamber or conclave.

The individual who is a secretary in very truth is a secretary according to the ancient Latin definition—a confidential officer. She is literally the understudy of an important executive. A high type secretary is a woman employed by a certain big financier, who is reputed to pay her $10,000 a year. Originally she was his stenographer—and an extraordinarily able stenographer. But she studied the business as thoroughly and carefully as she could. She was full of "commercial curiosity," eager to absorb every available bit of information, until she became a veritable second mind to her employer. She represents his view-point completely.

The secretary is a good amanuensis with an infinite capacity for details. It is her job to relieve her chief of every possible detail, so that his mind is kept unburdened for consideration of more vital concerns. She should have a good education and be able to supplement information occasionally. She keeps herself posted about many developments of business in which her chief may be interested; she sifts facts for him; can act for him in his absence; and is a buffer between him and time-wasting interruptions.

The best secretaryships are not to be had for the asking, but are jobs created by years of service. They are developed, rarely picked out of a "help wanted" column. The stenographer can develop her post into a secretarial job in many cases, but unless her promotion to the title of "secretary" carries with it increased responsibility and pay she is not a secretary in the real sense of the word. A stenographer who takes dictation from the president of the company is not a secretary just because she works for the most important official. On the other hand, if in addition to her duties as an amanuensis she is entrusted with the carrying out of responsible business missions; if she is expected to act for her chief in his absence, she is a secretary in the original definition of the word.

Being secretary to an important business man, while a splendid apprenticeship for a successful business career, need not always be regarded as the end and aim of the business woman. There are some pitfalls in this job for the really ambitious woman. The able secretary often acquires a belief that it is she who is handling the big job, when, as a matter of fact, she is merely the vehicle for carrying out instructions. Here is where the ambitious woman is likely to lose the habit of exercising initiative unless she is fortunate enough to have a post which calls this faculty into action constantly. And so, the more comfortable the secretaryship, the more likely is the woman to sink into it contentedly and fall asleep in her pleasant little job. The danger comes when, through some business upheaval, she loses her pleasant job with its big salary, and she is faced with the unthinkable certainty that she can't get another like it.

Here, for example, is a woman secretary who has been trained into her present important job by her chief. She is absolutely invaluable to him—truly his "right hand." She knows all about his affairs. Through ten years of association her mind has been trained to work just like his, and she has copied him so painstakingly that now she can decide with almost unfailing accuracy just what his judgment would be in an emergency. As an individual, however, she is unimaginative, unprogressive, and minus any distinctively strong characteristics, except indeed imitativeness. If she were to lose her job to-morrow, it is absolutely certain she could not get another like it, nor would she be able to earn half her present salary in any job. She would have to train ten years more in another organization before her mind would be a safe deposit vault fcr another group of valuable facts.

And so, this word of warning to the woman with executive ambitions. A secretaryship is to be regarded as a training-ground, not an ultimate goal. Even the secretary to the President of the United States does not regard his post as the apex of his career; rather it has been the beginning of bigger things.

XIII

ADVERTISING AND THE WOMAN WHO CAN WRITE

Two Southern girls walked into an advertising agency some years ago, carrying a few sketches and verses which they had written together. The drawings were unusual and catchy, the jingles amusing, and the advertising agent bought them for a small sum. But when the story leaked out that these drawings and verses, plastered over the entire country, were written by two inexperienced young girls, also that fabulous sums had been paid them for the effort, the advertising agent was besieged by ambitious men and women, eager to turn their hand to "ad-writing" so that they could begin buying country homes and steam yachts for themselves!

Indeed, in a not very remote past one agency made advertising capital out of the fact that they were "paying a copy-writer

$1,000 a week!" The many exaggerated tales woven around advertising have made it seem to the lay mind a sort of Aladdin's Lamp of business—all poetry and profit. And so we shall immediately throw a wet blanket on the proposition that advertising as a profession is a veritable gold mine by quoting herewith the annual salaries of some noted advertising managers. Out of 42 advertising managers only three received $7,500 a year, or more; four received $6,500 a year; six received $5,200 a year; three received $4,420 a year; eleven received $3,900 a year; fifteen received $3,200 a year, or less.[1]

There are over 8,000 general advertisers, most of whom employ some one to supervise their advertising, and it has been estimated that the average salary of an advertising manager is between $1,200 and $2,000 a year.

Nevertheless, there is no doubt that advertising offers many good opportunities and is a highly desirable occupation for the woman who has some writing ability, a good education, imagination, and much common

[1] Courtesy "Advertising & Selling."

sense. Business interests are more and more depending on advertising to carry their message to the people. Every business with a commodity or service to sell requires advertising. Advertising is used by the public service corporations to develop good will; even strikers, or corporations with a strike on hand buy advertising space to present their story and get a public judgment. Advertising is growing in importance because of these factors: (1) Better transportation facilities which make it possible for a manufacturer to distribute his product all over the country; (2) The growing faith of the public in advertising, because of the gradual elimination of fraudulent and misleading advertising; (3) The recognition that the product which withstands the limelight of advertising is a dependable product.

It is estimated that about 700 million dollars a year are spent on advertising, and it takes an army of 8,000 general advertisers, about 320 recognized advertising agents, about 23,000 periodicals and several hundred producers of other advertising media—billboards, painted display, novelties, signs, etc. —plus their staff to carry on this business.

Advertising may be defined as a tool with which information is spread. Its purpose is to influence public opinion. Mark this point, however: advertising is not just "ad-writing." The written advertisement is the finished expression by which the advertiser endeavors to reach the public. Beneath it is an intricate, interlocking organization—producing, distributing, and advertising machinery in well-adjusted cooperation.

Facing page 264 is a chart showing the *personnel* of the Advertising Department of a large national advertiser, and the duties of each member of the staff. What positions women hold in such a department, and their opportunities are discust later in the chapter.

NO. 7.—THE ROUTING OF AN ADVERTISING CAMPAIGN

1. *Personnel of Advertiser*.
   - President
   - Board of directors
   - General manager
   - Sales manager
   - Advertising manager

2. *Advertising Agency....*	Solicitor in charge of accounts Planning or promotion department Space-buyer Copy-writer Artist Buyer of printing Checkers, general office help
3. *Advertising Media.....*	Newspapers Magazines (popular, technical, trade and class) Street-cars Billboards, painted display and outdoor signs Electrical display Window-display Store demonstration Catalogs, circulars and follow-up letters Sampling House-to-house canvassing Novelties Programs "Stunt" advertising—like "Special weeks," exhibitions, contests and unusual dealer helps

Assume that a large advertiser is about to decide on his advertising appropriation for the ensuing year and to make his plans. What happens? As is customary in large organizations, the advertiser employs an "advertising manager" who is directly in charge of all publicity, also an "advertising agency." The agency consists of a group of specialists, individuals who plan campaigns, buy space in advertising media, write copy, and attend to the details of placing advertisements. About 90 per cent. of all general advertising copy is prepared or placed by agents.

The advertising manager, probably in co-operation with the agency, prepares a detailed statement showing the advertising done the previous year, supplemented by comparisons with other factors, *i.e.*, sales records, increased number of dealers, and any other conditions developed by advertising. It also includes an analysis of present conditions, the needs of the business, and a recommendation for a plan of advertising that will mean sales expansion.

The report is considered by the executives, or board of directors, and they decide what

(No. 8)—PERSONNEL OF AN ADVERTISING DEPARTMENT AND THEIR DUTIES

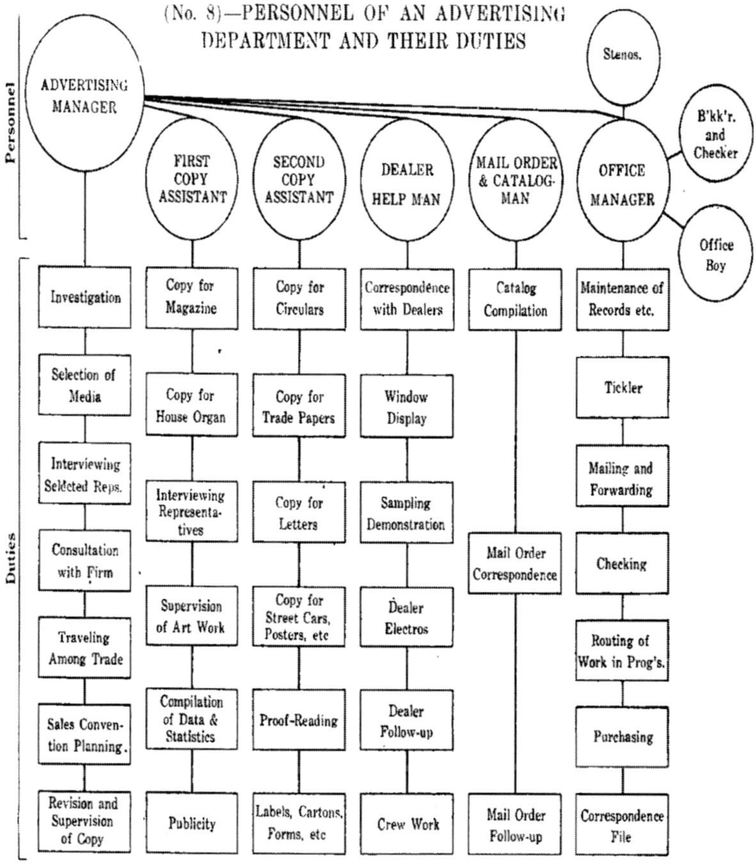

A chart representing the standard or ideal advertising department organization is now found very valuable in modern advertising departments, not because any such chart can be applied in its entirety, but because it serves as a guide in the gradual organization and development work.

The chart here illustrated represents the combined plans of a number of efficient advertising departments, and therefore appears to be an exceptionally large organization. However, the interrelation between the existing departments (even if fewer in number) and the advertising department is practically the same.

The relation in which the advertising department stands toward executives varies in different organizations, about as follows:

1. Advertising department subordinately connected with sales department;
2. Advertising department independently subordinate to general manager;
3. Advertising department co-equally subordinate with sales department to general manager or president or sales executive committee;
4. Advertising department subordinate to president or vice-president or board of directors, but not within the authority of any other department or executive.

In the accompanying chart the needs of the typical large national advertiser, using all types of media and selling through salesmen to retailers and by mail, have been considered.

Whether the line of authority shall be direct from the chief executive to the head of advertising department depends on whether the advertising is the most vital factor in sales, or purely an additional sales stimulus. For example, certain staples that have been sold for years through fixt channels do not depend on advertising. Many of such manufacturers advertise to the public only a certain branded article added to the line, the sales of which form only a very small percentage of the total volume of business. In such cases, executives are interested to only a secondary degree in the advertising, and the advertising staff cooperates with and reports to the sales department or some group of officials interested.

However, where the distribution of a product depends entirely on the demand created by advertising, the line of authority is direct from the chief executive to the advertising department head.

(Courtesy The Business Bourse, Int., Inc., New York.)

shall be the advertising policy and the amount of money spent. Sometimes they O. K. or select the actual media to be used. Very likely, they will base the appropriation on definite factors. Is the campaign for "direct returns," or for "educational work" or for general publicity?" The amount spent may be a fixt per cent. of the gross or net sales of the previous year; or, if a radical change in policy is contemplated, or there is exceptionally brisk competition to meet, or other complicated conditions have arisen, the appropriation may be an arbitrary sum, based on immediate needs and with no relation to previous business. Here are the reasons why any firm advertises:

(1) To educate the public about a new product and make its trade-mark familiar.
(2) As a check to decreased sales, especially in times of business depression.
(3) To meet competition.
(4) To enlarge the field of sales by advertising new and varied uses of an article.
(5) To counteract a wrong impression.
(6) To overcome the disadvantage of a "seasonal" demand by advertising new uses between seasons.

(7) To conquer the substitution evil.
(8) As a stimulus to greater dealer interest.
(9) To develop good will.
(10) For gathering a "family" of products under a single trade-mark, and so interchanging the benefits of good will and demand among a group of articles manufactured by the same firm.

What is called "general publicity" is advertising that is simply a reminder, a means of keeping the name of the advertiser in the public eye, but from which no direct returns are expected. Numbers 5, 7 and 9 might be called "general publicity." "Direct advertising," however, is a type of publicity which is planned for the purpose of selling goods at once. The reader is expected to send in his order to the manufacturer or a local dealer as an immediate result of the advertisement.

In addition, every advertising campaign of value includes some definite method of enlisting the cooperation and enthusiasm of dealers and salesmen if they are depended on to help the distribution plans. It is not long since both dealers and salesmen, in large numbers, felt antagonistic toward the whole scheme of advertising. Dealers declared very often that advertising only increased the cost of goods and cut into profits. Salesmen grumbled that, if the amount spent on advertising were added to their salaries they could get better results! With these two strong factors in selling opposed to advertising, it was no wonder that advertising was so costly and waste ran high!

But now the cooperation of salesmen with the advertising campaign is enlisted at the very beginning. At salesmen's conventions there are talks on the principles of advertising as well as information on the advertising of the house, so that salesmen of the modern type understand advertising and pass on their knowledge to customers. Several weeks before the beginning of an advertising campaign salesmen are supplied with loose-leaf books containing advance copies of advertisements, lists of periodicals in which they are to be inserted, other media to be used, and lists of "dealer helps"—booklets, or novelties, or special window trims or store displays. Some advertisers go so far as to supply complete showcases to dealers who order sufficiently large quantities. The opinion of salesmen (and dealers, too) is often asked about certain modes of advertising, and their recommendations or criticisms have due weight in advertising councils.

It will be seen from the foregoing that advertising to-day is a complicated industry, requiring broad business experience, knowledge of the distribution system, judgment of human nature, and a few other things besides writing ability. There is a great deal of information to be obtained before an advertisement is written — long before the eventful moment when a deliberative board of directors place their O. K. on a plan and appropriation.

"How can advertisers plan a correct line of action?" is often asked. Formerly much advertising was made up of guesswork, sudden brilliant ideas, and great faith in large appropriations. But a more scientific spirit has crept into advertising. Where men used to guess they now test, and the best type of advertising policy is the fruit of analysis and investigation. A certain progressive manufacturer, about to launch a new product, had a complete investigation made on the following lines before one dollar was spent on advertising:

(1) The article was tested for imperfections in manufacture by a number of technical experts.

(2) The article was tested by 200 women consumers to get their disinterested opinion, criticisms and suggestions.

(3) A study was made of the total consumption of similar commodities now on the market; what sections of the country were especially responsive; plans and methods of competitors; trade opinion of competitive products; skeleton outline of possible extended uses of the article not yet generally known.

(4) Expert opinion was obtained on the trade-mark; its suitability for foreign as well as American use; search made among unregistered as well as registered marks.

(5) Cost experts were called to estimate possible costs, expenditures, profits for dealers, and on the basis of their report a reasonable price was fixt.

It may seem expensive to obtain all this information before the product has been so much as offered in the market, but it has been found the least costly method in the long run. For example, the manufacturer of a kitchen device spent thousands of dollars trying to sell his machine, all to no purpose. If he had taken the trouble to consult a group of disinterested housewives, he would have learned at once the small technical imperfection that was, nevertheless, a definite handicap to sales; and he would have saved useless sales campaigns made before he had perfected his product. Another manufacturer of a costly business machine decided to investigate his market carefully before beginning an aggressive advertising campaign, and enlarging his factory. He learned that if he increased his daily output, as he planned, he would exhaust his market in two years, because the field was limited—and his profits would have been expended uselessly. An automobile manufacturer who had spent thousands of dollars popularizing his trade-mark found foreign advertising totally unresponsive, until a trade-mark expert pointed out that his trade-mark meant in Spanish, "criminal"—rather an unhappy choice for the name of an automobile.

Advertisers have learned that investigation before a campaign pays. Reports from salesmen and from special, trained investigators—a house-to-house canvass of consumers, tests on individuals in the psychological laboratory—these are the methods which prevail in the modern advertising organization. The progressive advertising manager doesn't order half a million pretty packages until he first has a few hundred sample packages "tried out" on dealers' shelves to see whether they really stand out from other products or are self-effacing, and whether they evoke compliment or criticism from dealer and consumer. Trade-marks, advertising slogans and even arguments which it is proposed to use in advertising copy, are tested on consumers or subjects in the psychologist's laboratory before adoption. In other words, successful advertising is the result of an infinite capacity to dig for facts.

There are three types of organizations in which the woman with advertising ambitions may find a place: (1) With an advertiser—

either a national advertiser, department store, or other retail merchandiser; (2) With an advertising agency; (3) With an advertising medium.

The advertising jobs open to her are: (1) Checker, stenographer, or other types of clerical work in the office of an advertiser, agency or medium; (2) Copy-writer; (3) Artist; (4) Space-buyer; (5) Buyer of printing, novelties, etc.; (6) Solicitor of advertising; (7) Advertising manager's assistant; (8) Advertising manager.

Many women who are to-day in the foremost ranks of advertising graduated into their present work from subordinate posts. One advertising woman who spends a million dollars a year for her firm began as a stenographer in the organization, then became assistant to the advertising manager, then buyer of printing, and finally advertising manager. There are few women who are advertising managers of large national distributors, altho there are somewhat more women who have charge of the advertising in retail and department stores. Women excel particularly in department and retail store advertising work, and many of them have the responsibility of the department, even tho the store does not deem it good policy to confer the title "advertising manager" upon them! S. Roland Hall, one of the authors of the I. C. S. course on advertising, and himself an advertising manager of note, declared, "It is my conviction that on account of the difference between man's and woman's point of view, and because so large a proportion of the necessities of life are bought by women (some put it as high as 80 per cent.) the usefulness of women ad-writers is sure to be recognized more generally."

The reason for the lack of women advertising managers of national organizations is probably the same as for the lack of men who are advertising managers in the biggest sense. The highest type advertising manager is the man who has a broad foundation of business experience, first-hand selling knowledge, knowledge of the principles and problems of modern distribution, ability to make analysis. Very often he travels over the country, visiting dealers so that he knows exactly what trade conditions are, and how to apply the advertising tonic to stimulate sluggish distribution wherever needed. It might seem that woman can not do all this. But many men can not or will not, and a large number of them are "advertising managers in name only." Literally, they are purchasing clerks.

The advertising manager who fulfils completely the functions of his calling is a business analyst and counsel as well as a buyer of space and writer of copy. He knows the market, varying conditions throughout the country, competition conditions, from first-hand contact and travel. There are some exceptionally clever women who do this work also—women who know how to analyze the trade, make consumer investigations, and formulate campaigns on the basis of first-hand facts. There is no reason why the able woman with fine ambitions can not equip herself for an advertising manager's job in its complete sense.

The best way to get training is to obtain a position in an advertising department—any kind of position, even if it is only to file electrotypes or check advertisements—anything to keep in an advertising atmosphere. This experience is supplemented by a course of study—and there are good courses available in many of the colleges, high schools, correspondence schools. The woman who is a stenographer has a special advantage, for advertising plans, "copy," and correspondence about rates, will come to her and give her a daily education.

In the advertiser's office she may become a buyer of space (if the advertiser is one of the few who places copy direct with publications instead of through an agency), or she may become the buyer of printing, plates, papers, etc., for catalogs, folders and other accessories. Women are good "shoppers," and thus good buyers of advertising material. The work is well paid, some experienced women in large organizations receiving from $30 to $100 a week, depending on the size of the advertising appropriation.

If she has writing ability distinctly and her ambitions are definitely toward writing, she may become a "copy-writer"—that is, the person who actually writes the finished advertisement as we see it in print. In smaller organizations the woman copy-writer is expected to be advertising manager as well—having charge of the buying of space, the printing, the selection of media, etc. Copy-writing presents the biggest field in advertising for women to-day. Woman's native knowledge of how to appeal to consumers, a woman's better knowledge of merchandise, her natural talkativeness which makes her a better descriptive writer than a man, all develop what one advertising expert calls a "natural-born copy-writer." There is little difference between the salaries paid men and women copy-writers; and the sums vary from $25 to $100 a week, according to personal ability.

But the woman of marked ability in writing advertising copy, and also the woman who is a specially shrewd buyer of space, is likely to gravitate toward the agency, because of the limited number of big positions open in advertisers' offices. The agencies, on the other hand, employ a regular staff of writers, solicitors, and one or more space buyers, and therefore provide a wider opportunity.

The higher posts in an advertising agency are: (1) Copy-writer; (2) Space-buyer; (3) Solicitor. Sometimes the solicitor is also expected to write copy, but this plan has not met with much success. The agency solicitor is supposed to be a first-class salesman with ideas for business development; and altho he can often criticize copy, he has not, as a rule, any ability to write good copy himself. And so the common custom is for the solicitor to secure advertising accounts, the space buyer to "place" advertising, and the copy-writer to write the actual advertisement.

Women have been employed as copy-writers in advertising agencies, and as the woman view-point is important in the preparation of advertising (most of which is read by women) they often receive preference over men writers. Writing copy in an advertising agency requires a good education, considerable versatility and imagination, and a well-developed facility in expression. The copy-writer may be expected to visit the factory of the advertiser, and to absorb information about manufacturing processes, so that she may gather points and present a strong, attractive, convincing story. So she needs, in addition to writing ability, a "nose for news," so to speak; an ability to detect the unusual, the interesting, the novel points that people like to read about, and which may have utterly escaped the manufacturer, so close to his product that he has no viewpoint about it.

The purpose of an advertisement has been summarized as follows: (1) To attract attention; (2) Sustain interest; (3) Carry conviction; (4) Induce action. It requires knowledge of a product, education in psychology, plus an ability for sincere and convincing presentation to make an advertisement successful. The most perfect English is futile if it is hackneyed argument. Similarly, the wild effort to be original at any cost sometimes produces colossal absurdities that are an insult to the intelligence of the public. But here, too, the pet slogan of the modern advertiser will prove the guide and salvation of the ingenious copy-writer. Dig for facts. Play on the imagination. Try to ally your arguments with some human interest point—or a subject of popular interest. It can be done. What is more difficult to advertise than books? In every magazine dozens of pages compete for your attention to tell how very much better educated you will be, how your evenings will be full of entertainment, etc., if you will only buy "our wonderful set of Thackeray"—or the "Life of General Grant," or the "Home Encyclopedia of Useful Knowledge." We pass the hackneyed advertisement that yearns to elevate or reform us, but our attention is arrested by a "human-natured" advertisement that sold thousands of sets of O. Henry's stories. This pictured two men and a bride in tears, and bore the caption, "And these three did not meet again for 20 years!" Incidentally, that advertisement and the whole series of which it was a part, were prepared by a woman. One should dig for the point of human interest, the feature that distinguishes the product from competitive goods, or the unusual service that is offered. Every business has a note of individuality somewhere even if it is successfully concealed. Search for that distinctive note and play on it interestingly in your copy, and you will have an audience.

The "space buyer" in the advertising agency is an encyclopedia of information on advertising media, their circulation and rates. (See third group in Chart 7.) Few women occupy this post, altho women who are advertising managers sometimes have also the responsibility of buying space. Nevertheless, this is a position that an intelligent woman can train for, because it requires the keen "shopping" type of mind to be a good space buyer.

Through the activities of the Advertisers' Audit Association, the job of space buyer has been rendered somewhat easier. This organization makes an actual audit of periodicals, and then places the facts about circulation within reach of A. A. A. members. As can be realized, this is an improvement over the ancient condition, where publications would claim a large circulation, charge a high rate in consequence, and advertisers would dispute the claim. But neither side had proof.

As far as rates are concerned, space buying has its difficulties. Most publications claim to have a fixt rate—a "one-price system" so to speak—and to stick to their rate card. Some of them do. But for certain types of publications, the space buyer works on the supposition that he can always get a lower rate. For example, the rate card offers a 5 per cent. discount for a

5,000-line order. One space buyer, working on the reasonable assumption that some periodicals can always be tempted with a real order, attached his check to an order for 2,000 lines at the 5,000-line rate and it was accepted.

This condition is gradually being eliminated, but it still exists to some extent.

So it will be seen that the space buyer can not rest content with the acquisition of a few facts, but must keep on seeking more and more information and keeping up-to-the-minute on facts about changes in all sorts of advertising media. Really good space buyers who are thoroughly informed, are exceedingly rare, and they are paid anywhere from $40 a week up.

Many fashion publications, trade papers in textile fields, and some newspapers employ women to solicit advertising. The agencies, however, rarely employ women as solicitors—also for reasons of prejudice, not for lack of ability in women. The solicitor for an agency, to be really successful, must be able to "build accounts." That is to say, he seeks out a manufacturer and by getting facts about his product, distribution, and selling problems in some fashion, is able to suggest ideas for a plan of sales expansion. Of course, there is more or less of a scramble among advertising agents to get established big accounts by offering better service; but the constructive side of solicitation, and the hardest kind of work, is the building of new accounts. There are agencies which fifteen or twenty years ago began tiny advertising campaigns for some obscure manufacturers, but who have worked unceasingly developing accounts, which today are national advertisers whose annual appropriation for publicity runs near the million-dollar mark.

As can be seen, it is necessary for the solicitor to gain the confidence of a manufacturer, and to get full facts about his business—and it is difficult work for a woman to persuade some types of business men that she can increase business for them! There are women who do this, however, and who have literally "put on the map" food products, textiles, etc., that were unknown before. The solicitor has imagination, sound business judgment, and is well informed about modern methods of distribution, including ample data about plans that will not work. A good solicitor is the backbone of an advertising agency. Some men who have made good as solicitors have been made part owners of the agency they serve. It is, therefore, obvious that the able advertising woman, with selling ability, can find in this work the road to semi-proprietorship, if not complete ownership, eventually, of an agency.

Several women are, to-day, owners of advertising agencies—an interesting but exceedingly difficult business. Most advertising agencies are supported by the 10 or 15 per cent. which media pay them for turning in business. In other words, if an advertiser spends $150,000 a year in publications, the agency which places this business draws a commission that may vary from $15,000 downward. But the commission system of payment has flaws. In the first place, an advertising agency must be "recognized" by the American Newspaper Publishers' Association before any periodical will pay it a commission. Before recognition is secured, the agent must prove to the satisfaction of this organization that he has a certain number of bona fide accounts; that his business per annum will amount to the minimum fixt by the organization; that he is not the advertising manager of any of his clients (which would subject him to the suspicion that he is secretly splitting commissions with the firm he serves). There are approximately 1,800 advertising agents in the country; but less than 400 are "recognized" by the A. N. P. A.

The great objection to the commission system of payment is that very often the amount paid is in inverse ratio to the amount of service rendered. An agency may be giving especially good service but doing uphill work for a manufacturer who is just beginning to advertise. Because his appropriation is small, the agent receives a smaller sum in commission than he would if the concern was well established, had a smooth-running advertising department of its own, and a large appropriation. For this reason more and more agencies are shifting to the "fee and contract" form rather than the commission basis. These agents estimate the amount of work a client will require, and agree to handle the advertising for a fixt sum per year, making extra charges for extra items, but turning over to the advertiser the commissions which media pay. This system also removes suspicion from the mind of advertisers who sometimes assumed that agents counseled large appropriations because the larger the appropriation the larger the commission drawn by the agent. Under the "fee and contract" system, the agent receives the fees agreed upon on a basis of service rendered and not according to the size of the advertising appropriation.

The whole subject of recognition and payment of agents is now being reconsidered by the various advertising media and the advertising agents and changes in the system are being contemplated

It takes a great many years to build solid advertising accounts and sustained effort to keep them. But there is no reason why the woman with merchandising information and creative ability can not go into the field and eventually establish herself in an advertising agency of her own. There are several women who own advertising agencies and have developed big accounts. The very fact that she is a woman will help her when she comes to plan campaigns to reach women consumers. She knows the woman view-point, she knows how women buy, what they like, what they do not like, and what appeals win them best.

As far as soliciting for periodicals and other advertising media is concerned, this is a large field, practically untouched by women. A few women on the typically women's publications earn very large salaries—because they are good salespeople. They know how to present logical, convincing arguments, supported by facts and statistics, to prove that the paper represented has the right kind of circulation to be a favorable medium for their prospective advertiser's wares. This may lead to the post of advertising manager for the periodical—at present a man's job.

It is a cheerful fact that every modern business of any consequence requires the services of some one, constantly or periodically, to do good writing. Chief among industries requiring women who can write are the mail-order houses. There are about 35 really large mail-order houses in the country (most of them located in the largest cities), but since the possibilities of mail-order have become more generally known, hundreds of retail and department stores have established a "mail-order department" which, in a smaller way, operates along the same lines as the large mail-order concerns.

Mail-orders depend largely on a skilful pen. No buying is done in an attractive salesroom, where the personality of the saleswoman is depended on to influence a decision. The mail-order house transplants personality into the pages of a catalog, into written advertisements, daily correspondence. Its prosperity depends on whether that written matter is alive, enticing, interesting and convincing. There are two branches of mail-order work for the woman writer. One is to dictate replies to customers—answering inquiries, adjusting difficulties, and keeping the good will of the customer at any cost. Consequently, the work requires idea-fulness, optimism, and facility. It may be said that mail-order work is excellent schooling for the woman with advertising aspirations. It exercises her mind, develops fertility of ideas and quickens her facility in writing. If she is alert enough to keep out of a rut by conscious effort, she can build an original style of her own. There is a certain stimulation about mail-order correspondence in that the results are traceable. It is possible to know definitely in very many cases just what letter produced orders, because mail-order writing is distinctively advertising that must produce direct returns.

Correspondence work in a mail-order organization requires a high school or college education, because it demands a knowledge of psychology, ability to concentrate, and fluent diction. But it often happens that a woman with an elementary education, possest of an ability at expression and a knowledge of human nature learned through business experience, proves to be just as capable as the college woman.

Correspondence work in a mail-order house does not bring high compensation. Women rarely receive more than $25 per week; and the average salaries paid are between $14 and $20. This is due partly to the fact that some mail-order houses can do their correspondence on "forms," so that a $10 clerk can be trained to pick out paragraphs from good form letters and answer letters intelligently. It is also because many correspondence positions are filled by educated women thrown suddenly on their own resources, and glad to do any paying work which savors of intelligent effort.

Mail-order correspondence work, therefore, is not sufficiently large as an end to the ambitious woman, but it is splendid training. Some women have developed from correspondents to the second branch of mail-order work—the preparation of the all-important catalog. These catalogs are really marvelous affairs, sometimes several hundred pages in length. Women have been found especially expert in preparing the writing matter, and giving descriptions of articles that are illustrated. As catalogs are issued twice a year, and sometimes oftener, and are always supplemented by hundreds of special folders and leaflets, this occupation affords regular work to the woman in the advertising department.

There are women who have become so expert in this work that they do it independently—"free-lance work," as it is called. Some of them will do nothing but prepare a catalog for a mail-order merchant, write the copy, and supervise the illustrating, printing, etc. Occasionally an exceptionally experienced and able woman will even help in the selection of merchandise that is especially suitable for mail-order trade. She thus is really the brains of a mail-order house—buying merchandise, and managing the presentation of it to possible buyers so that the business grows.

There are many opportunities open to a woman correspondent in the office of any large organization. She may create a post in the sales department, answering salesmen's inquiries, and writing "follow-up" sales letters to dealers. The credit and collection department requires some one to write strong, effective, but diplomatic letters to customers for past due accounts. In the complaint and adjustment department, she may be required to write polished epistles that will smooth the ruffled feelings of an outraged customer. All of this work is the best kind of training for the determined woman of ability, intent on improving her craftsmanship in writing, and enlarging her store of business information. For her it is the entering wedge to bigger opportunities.

A few hints may help her in her progress.

First, she must possess, in addition to an ability to write, a fund of optimism, and the habit of affirmation rather than negation. In good letter-writing the constructive side must be emphasized.

Second, she must have an ever-inquiring mind. She is naturally interested in human nature, and as sympathetic with the yearnings of the farmer's wife in a tiny rural community as in the doings of the fashionable metropolitan woman.

Third, she must interest herself more than superficially in the business she is serving. Her opportunity lies in not only studying her business, but the organization as a whole and the entire industry as it is developing and changing.

Fourth. Letters should have a personal touch, but one can not always "write just as you talk," as is so often advised. Familiarities, jokes, exaggerated expressions of esteem may bubble over in a personal talk and be entirely acceptable and even relished. But they convey a different impression when they appear in print. They seem offensive and patently insincere, and you can not afford to be insincere, even if it is only to a poor farm woman, saving her butter-and-egg money with which to buy a new suit. She is interested in knowing how much she can get for how little money, and she will read a very long letter that gives her this information in detail, in a natural, readable, courteous way. Friendly feelings are created in the customer by personal service—not merely by friendly expressions. Tell her something real, give her detailed information about the things she wants to know, be helpful and interesting, and she is yours.

The woman who develops ability in effective business writing may become a specialist, doing "free-lance" work for which there is a limited but growing field. She may write booklets, catalogs, form letters, etc., for a large number of firms. She can help out by writing for "trade papers," or house organs, or even edit house organs in their entirety. There is a definite field for writing original, or "newsy," articles for the trade papers which always welcome new ideas. Free-lance work is as difficult in business as in strictly literary fields until a reputation is achieved. The woman who starts doing free-lance work will find that it is much easier to write a brilliant form letter or booklet than to get an order for it at a good price.

The best step for her is to make herself a specialist on some one subject before she launches into the field of independent business writing. She may have a special ability that she can capitalize, and make herself an authority on some one subject—textiles or fashions, or foods, or household equipment, or interior decorations. She will then be able to write material that contains valuable information for the reader, and so much more desirable to incorporate in copy for an advertiser.

Following is an outline of a Course in Advertising, as arranged for the use of schools, clubs and Y. M. C. A.'s by Frank Leroy Blanchard, of the Educational Committee of the Associated Advertising Clubs of the World:

1. The Advertising Field—What it offers in the way of a career; how to obtain instruction.
2. A Brief History of Advertising—Ancient advertising. Description of modern advertising media.
3. The "Ad-Writer" and His Work—Broad edu-

cation and writing ability necessary—also knowledge of article, audience and selling principles.

4. How to "Lay Out" an Advertisement—Rules of form, typography, etc.
5. On the Use of Illustrations.
6. What You Should Know About Paper, Type and Ink.
7. How to Advertise a Retail Business.
8. Department Store Advertising.
9. Problems of the General Advertiser—(As distinguished from retail advertiser.)
10. Selling Goods by Mail.
11. Fakes and Follies of the Advertising Field.
12. Functions of the Advertising Agency.
13. The Advertising Solicitor — Qualifications, training and compensation.
14. Canvassing the Field—System and ethics of successful soliciting.
15. Closing the Contract—Common sense and etiquette of interviewing prospective clients.
16. The Advertising Manager—Classes of advertising managers; qualifications.
17. Newspapers as Advertising Mediums—Value for quick-fire publicity work; how to use small and large space.
18. Value of Magazines as Business Builders.
19. When to Use Trade and Class Papers.
20. The Appeal of Street-Car Advertising.

21. Outdoor Advertising.
22. Circulars, Booklets and Catalogs—Their preparation, cost and distribution.
23. Letters, Novelties, Follow-up Schemes, Tracing Results.
24. Truth in Advertising—What the A. A. C. of W. has done to eliminate misrepresentations in advertising; advertising laws.

XIV

WHOLESALE OR OUTSIDE SELLING; THE "TRAVELING SALESWOMAN"

"You can easily make $15 a week in spare time," she was told. "Mrs. Smith, our agent, earned $200 in one single week." This statement is accompanied by an alleged photograph of Mrs. Smith. Advertisements thus worded attract into outside sales, or agency work, thousands of women who have neither ability nor inclination for the work, and whose chief asset is a desire to earn money. These advertisements may be scrupulously truthful. But it must not be supposed that because Mrs. Smith earned $200 in one week selling subscriptions that any one can do it; nor that $200 a week represents Mrs. Smith's regular weekly earnings at the work. Mrs. Smith is probably an experienced saleswoman and a "hustler," and has spent a long time preparing the ground for her brilliant success. It takes time and training to succeed in outside selling, but it is a desirable calling for women in many respects. In the first place, it is interesting work, and if sensible rules of living are observed, more healthful than many indoor occupations. In the second place, the work is highly profitable to a woman of ability, and she can make her earnings rise in proportion to her ability. Last, but not least, her personal contact with the trade or with the consumer, and her intimate knowledge of conditions are the finest equipment for the woman who plans to own a business eventually.

Outside selling may be divided into three classes: (1) Canvassing or outside selling direct to consumers; (2) Wholesale selling to the trade. The "canvasser" calls on any one and every one, with the hope of making prospective customers. "House-to-house canvass" is a familiar term, meaning just what it says—actually calling on every one in some town or district, visiting from house to house. The salesman is supposed to call on prospective customers only, altho sometimes a salesman "canvasses" for new trade also. When he does this it is called "missionary work." As a rule, however, the salesman is a better trained, more experienced person than the "canvasser," and, as his services are more valuable, his time is confined to calling on firms or individuals who have been interested in the proposition by a "canvasser" or by some form of advertising.

Salesmen, to approach consumers directly, are required for high-priced commodities, such as real estate, pianos, cash registers, typewriters and other office appliances; and to sell service, such as a course of study, advertising service, personal counsel, books, insurance, etc.

The second class of "outside selling" is the selling of merchandise to the retail trade—the familiar "traveling salesman." The word "sales*man*" is used because this manner of selling is as yet confined almost entirely to men. There are comparatively few women as yet who have entered the field of wholesale selling. The fascinating "Emma McChesney," made famous by Edna Ferber, is not a type by any means, but a very exceptional and somewhat fanciful even tho realistic personality. But women are cordially received in this field, and it is significant that in the World's Salesmanship Congress in Detroit (July, 1916), a special place for women sellers was made on the program.

In this chapter we shall consider the various branches of outside sales work, the possibilities they offer to women, what women have already done in this field, and how the salesmen of modern organizations (who may be used as a guide to women in this work) are selected and equipped for successful selling.

The retail or "inside" saleswoman serves a customer who voluntarily enters the store in a buying frame of mind. In other words, the retail saleswoman is sought by the customer. But the woman who sells outside must seek her customer. If she is supposed to do "canvassing" she has no customers at all—simply a list of names, or a city block, which she "canvasses" in order to find who are the possible buyers, or the "prospects," the business term for prospective customers. It is part of her work to create demand, whereas the saleswoman inside the store simply supplies an existing demand intelligently. It is important to recognize the difference between the inside and the outside saleswoman, because the outside saleswoman requires all the good qualities of the retail saleswoman, plus a few others.

In the first place, she needs to possess exuberant vitality—not merely the good health of the girl who boasts that she is never sick —because the nature of her work, the strain of travel, the necessity of imparting enthusiasm and creating interest where none exists, make enormous drains on her physique. As the first impression is a physical picture, the successful saleswoman must have a fine presence, must look prosperous, dignified and optimistic. She radiates success and enthusiasm—and carries this enthusiasm artistically and with restraint. Many earnest women overdo it. They are effervescent, and bubble over with so many bright ideas and engage in such brilliant conversation that the customer becomes bewildered—and a garrulous solicitor is a lost hope.

Another common handicap to women who sell outside is that they can be sidetracked by flattery. This grows out of a curious situation. From the actual experience of women solicitors, it may be said definitely that, so far from their occupation subjecting them to indignity, women who sell outside are the recipients of the greatest courtesy, except in rare instances. A saleswoman will be received by important men (either out of courtesy or a curiosity to see what she's like) where a salesman, equally able, can not penetrate further than the third assistant secretary.

A comparison of results for salesmen and saleswomen in the same fields shows an evident distinction in final results which proceeds more from difference in personality than ability. There is no denying the fact that the outside saleswoman is as yet so uncommon that her femininity is part of the atmosphere. Men do not like to "turn down" a saleswoman, and so a frequent complaint made by women who sell is that the customer who is pleasant and even enthusiastic over every argument she makes is the poorest "prospect" for a sale! It is a common trick for a business man who is not interested, or who remains indifferent to the proposition, to divert the conversation from the sales article to the personality of the woman solicitor, an inoffensive, and indeed flattering, method of "letting her down easy." The inexperienced woman, either because she is vain enough to want flattery, or because she deems it politic to humor her prospect, will allow the conversation to wander, and before she is aware the hearing is over and she has missed her sale. But the more experienced women learn how to make the most of their slight sex advantage. They use it to get a hearing, and they know how to eliminate digressions, and how, adroitly and tactfully, to bring back a wandering customer to the business in hand.

But, because of this condition, there exists among men who hire salespeople for outside work a conviction that women are "good to approach a buyer and pave the way, but they do not 'close' well." A man may not be able to get a hearing so easily, but "once he gets a hearing, he is more likely to close the sale quickly." A piano firm with a fine selling staff made excellent use of this fact. Women were employed as "canvassers"; they interviewed possible customers, produced pleasant impressions and obtained facts regarding the customers, but they made no attempt to sell; they merely paved the way for a salesman to follow and close the sale.

The second important qualification for successful selling is a generous equipment of facts. Women social workers are accustomed to quote facts and statistics; and business men use statistics ceaselessly. But few business women seem to use spontaneously the greatest lever in business, facts and figures. The statistical fact is more and more becoming an idol in modern business. Years ago the star salesman was the man who could entertain, or orate, or joke his customer into signing on the dotted line. But gone is the storekeeper who will spend a morning over the cracker barrel listening to the "drummer's" funny stories. Competition is keener than ever, and before the modern dealer gives an order he wants to know the "reason why." He must be shown facts about profits and selling cost, manufacturing superiority and, most of all, how he can make more money. In addition, the modern salesman knows business psychology. He knows when to base his arguments on different appeals—more profit, more power or more prestige—and how to adjust his argument to the temperament of possible customers.

There is too often a tendency among women who sell to place their faith in "intuition" and in an expected "sudden inspiration." But only trustworthy facts about her own business, about competition, about the "prospect's" business, about the industry in general, will make her always fearless of argument, quite sure of herself, and ready to formulate logical replies, even if she does not work from a stereotyped "selling talk." Pre-analysis is bringing selling almost to the level of a science. But depending on intuition, bursting on a "prospect" uninformed, and trusting to the luck of the day, lower selling to a point where it becomes nothing more than peddling. Training and preparation professionalize any work.

Two new opinions have risen in regard to what is the highest efficiency in selling. One is the conviction that "salesmen are made, not born," the second the possibility of developing salesmen. The old idea was to have one or two "star" salesmen to balance the results of plodders down on the lower rungs of the ladder. But the modern organization does not seek a "wonder-salesman," who, in previous years, practically held the whole business in the hollow of his hand. The idea now is to institute plans that will develop a staff of salesmen of even ability, a good general average being more stable than an organization composed of extremes of ability.

As a consequence, men are more carefully selected and more carefully trained for selling in the best organizations. The old plan of welcoming all comers to try their hand at selling has been discarded, because "hiring and firing" is recognized as one of the big leaks in business. Sales applicants are studied carefully, or put through tests (like the Scott tests described in Chapter II.) or some definite analytical method is used. A shrewd sales manager with years of experience in selecting men will formulate a regular system for selecting good timber. Or an applicant may have to spend several weeks in the training-school which is part of the sales department. His standing in school work will determine whether he is to be given an opportunity to go out and sell the firm's products. Even then he does not immediately go out and sell by himself, but accompanies an older salesman and spends a few weeks in "apprentice" work.

In other words, an organization worth

one's while to join checks up a man's potential ability before engaging him, and so saves both the man and the company the time and expense of useless experimentation. Where all applicants are welcomed, when every one who wants to is allowed to go out and "represent" the company, it is a signal either that competition is very keen and the company depends on sheer force of numbers to attain sales, in which case vigorous work is expected of the salesman, or it may indicate (as do the thousands of "agents wanted" advertisements published continuously) that the proposition is so poor it is picked up and dropt with equal rapidity, and the "sales force" is a perpetually shifting procession.

Suppose a man has been accepted as an addition to the sales force. No matter how good a salesman he may have been for some other organization, there is some kind of training in store for him before he can begin active work on his new job. It isn't true that "a good salesman can sell anything." Because a man has been a popular and successful salesman in the tobacco trade is no proof that he will be equally successful in selling advertising space, real estate, life insurance or adding machines. Of course, it is possible for a salesman to change from one type of work to some other and succeed, provided there is a proper preliminary training, so that the individual can have time to let new facts seep in and prepare to adjust himself to new conditions. To make this point clearer it might be well to consider types of products that are sold, and the character of men who succeed best in each. There are four kinds of marketable wares:

(1) *Staples*—Groceries, dry goods, textiles, drugs, hardware, shoes, furniture, or raw materials.

(2) *Specialties*—These are the semi-luxuries and patented articles—pianos, automobiles, office appliances, and patented labor-savers for the household.

(3) *Service*—Advertising agent, publications which sell space, efficiency engineers, those who operate schools or educational courses, are all sellers of service.

(4) *Property and Investment*—Stocks, bonds, real estate, insurance, bank accounts.

It has been found that men develop specific temperaments through selling certain types of wares. The "staples" salesman may be a conscientious, unimaginative plodder and be highly successful because of his particular brand of stick-to-it-iveness. But he is wholly unlike the "specialties" salesman, who has not quite so dependable a market. The specialties salesman is very often required to "create" a market where none exists—to do missionary work. For this he requires imagination, enthusiasm and more personal electricity, so that he can change indifference and galvanize interest. The "service" salesman is unlike the two first types. He is more mental, the most imaginative of all, and probably the most intellectual. The seller of staples, or of specialties, can produce samples, and in concrete ways arouse the customer's interest. But the service salesman depends for success on the skilfulness with which he can paint a word picture, and on the strength of his personality to influence favorable decision.

The seller of property is a somewhat different type. He is the shrewd, substantial individual, and his main asset is his ability to create confidence. The brilliant but erratic type of salesman who might succeed in selling service or specialties has the qualities which might make him exceptionally difficult to train as a seller of real estate or financial securities. His very brilliance might make him savor too much of the fictional stock salesman, or the clever "gold-brick" agent, or the "green goods man" of former days.

An illustration in point is that of a charming woman who sold service in a certain educational agency. She came in contact with many men and women, and her wit and attractive personality made her exceptionally successful. Her remarkable ability came to the attention of an official in a financial house, and she accepted an attractive offer from him to sell securities. Here she failed utterly. The reason was perfectly obvious. When she sold service her charm and conversational facility enabled her to present attractive pictures that influenced a favorable decision. But she had not been schooled for her new work. She had not been enlightened as to the different needs of stock selling—that it required stability, not brilliance; facts, not charming conversation; sound, dignified argument, not pleasant chatter.

This does not mean that the individual who has sold one type of commodity is not able to sell some other thing; but simply that the need for training must be recognized, and systematic methods of training adopted, if new salespeople are to succeed. Details of methods used by progressive organizations to train salesmen are given in Chapter VI., but they may be listed broadly as follows:

(1) School instruction; actual classroom work at the company's school; lectures by sales experts or department heads, either at headquarters or at branch salesrooms.

(2) Correspondence instruction; sales course; or sales manual giving arguments, replies to objections, etc.

(3) Field demonstration by sales manager or experienced men. Continued interest in sales instruction is maintained through the medium of:

(4) House organ, and intermittent bulletins on selling practise, technical side of product, advertising, new projects or policies contemplated.

(5) Regular conventions of salesmen at headquarters.

Because of the many equitable remuneration systems prevailing, outside selling is one of the few fields where compensation rises almost automatically in proportion to ability. The individual with selling ability can always find a market for her services and sell her services at a good price, because a good seller is a producer and an investment, not an expense to a business. There is no limit to the possible earnings of a good salesman or saleswoman. There are some high type salesmen who are so able that they refuse to work on any but a "straight commission" basis; and on that basis they earn more than many of the officials in the corporation they serve. The types of payment for salesmen are:

(1) Salary, plus expenses.

(2) Salary and commission, salesman paying his own expenses.

(3) Small salary, commission and expenses.
(4) "Straight commission" (usually with a "drawing account," which really is an advance against commissions).
(5) Any of these methods, plus a bonus.

The method which seems to grow more and more in favor with the modern sales organization is the "salary and bonus" plan. Under straight salary or straight commission basis of payment, it is often impossible to compensate the entire staff with equal justice, because of variations in territory. The custom of paying a flat salary or uniform commission to every man, whether he travels in metropolitan sections, where there are hundreds of customers within a radius of a few miles, or whether he "covers" less populous regions, where he has to spend two-thirds of his time traveling and only one-third in actual work, can not always be satisfactory. But, if there is a bonus paid, due consideration is given to the peculiar factors of each territory or "selling zone" in fixing each separate bonus. There are conditions under which a salesman might distinguish himself, even tho his actual sales do not mount to a spectacular figure. The commission system can not take care of these factors, but the bonus system does. Here is a typical method of operating a bonus system:

(1) The sales department makes an estimate of the amount of business that can be expected from each territory covered by a salesman. This is based on total consumption of product, the business it produced in previous years, plus a reasonable proportion of the total increase of business expected for the ensuing year. This figure is called a "quota," and may be represented by "points." The total sales of the company are represented by 100 points, part of which is allotted to each territory.

(2) But in fixing this "quota" other factors than actual sales may be considered in each case, *i.e.*,

(*a*) Character of territory; whether it is a new field, where "missionary work" is required; proportion of urban and rural population, and hence time that will be wasted in travel, if traveling costs are higher, etc.

(*b*) Character of population; illiterates, or low per capita of wealth, etc.

(*c*) Local competition. There are certain parts of the country where the company's competitors may be very firmly entrenched, because of their priority, or nearness to the local market, etc. Consequently, every new dealer and sale is a greater victory than if made in more favorable sections. The work is more difficult, requiring better salesmanship than many men who might produce more elsewhere possess.

(*d*) The number of new dealers which each member of the sales staff is expected to secure.

(*e*) Expected increase of sales over the previous year's record.

(*f*) Percentage of profit which sales should produce.

(This is a factor often used by concerns which sell some "special" on which there is little or no profit, but which is attractive to dealers on account of its low price. Consequently, it is manufactured in order to give salesmen an "opening wedge" for other orders. As it is usually a very easy article to sell, the men are prevented from concentrating on it. They are penalized by getting little or no credit or commission on the "special," and this decreases the amount of the bonus paid for all sales.)

(*g*) Percentage of returned goods, or complaints about misunderstanding or misrepresentation of terms.

In the modern organization salesmen are restrained from encouraging a dealer to "stuff" his order. The salesman who induces a dealer to stock more goods than he can handle is no longer given a reward, but a reprimand for "overloading." Salesmen know after experience that it is better to book a small order, so that the dealer will have to order frequently (thus getting the impression that the stock is moving fast), than to book an order larger than the dealer's capacity. If goods remain on his shelves from one season to another, the dealer gets an idea that they are "slow sellers," and wishes to return them. The modern idea is not to "make a sale of any kind," but "make a good sale, or none at all." There is an incalculable loss in the sacrifice of a dealer's good will through overloading, and it can not be repaid by any temporary profit on an order.

Either semi-annually or annually the results of each salesman's territory are totaled, and the salesman is paid a bonus on the basis of his "quota." The bonus may be a similar *percentage* applied to every man's account. The actual *amount* paid to each man will vary, according to whether he has reached, or exceeded his quota, and by how much.

Earlier in the chapter it was pointed out that this is a field in which there are as yet few women. Can women succeed in outside selling or as "traveling saleswomen?" Women have succeeded in this work, and it is one of the higher, more responsible, and more profitable occupations which women of brains and ambition are sure to enter. True, it is difficult work. But all profitable occupations are difficult—difficult for men, too, and if we desire a man's pay we will have to be ready to undertake a "man-size job."

As a matter of fact, there are some lines of outside selling in which women can outreach men, just because they are women. There are manufacturers of corsets and women's apparel generally who train women, in preference to men, to sell their products. The reason is obvious. That women are especially shrewd merchandisers of women's wear is indicated strongly by the fact that the majority of buyers for big retail stores are women. It is, therefore, reasonable to suppose that women can be trained to be equally successful in the selling of women's merchandise in a bigger way.

There are other types of outside selling in which women have distinguished themselves—the selling of real estate, insurance, service, books, magazines, subscriptions, etc. It is a common fact that, in the buying of real estate for a home the wife may have a stronger influence than the husband in making the decision, even tho the man pays the bills. It is she who lives in the home entirely, and so there are many points which enter into her consideration that a man would leave out. A woman understands best a woman's view-point, and women who sell real estate are shrewd enough to first win the cooperation of the wife of a prospective purchaser by introducing into their sales talk the arguments which appeal to a woman, but which may escape a man altogether—such as the local social status, the facilities for school, the facilities for marketing. In selling a house the real estate saleswoman dwells on the utilitarian conveniences of kitchen and service portions, arrangement of rooms, light, heat, that the homemaker must consider and which win her approval. In view of the ever-widening influx of city dwellers into rural and suburban districts, and the fact that country living is becoming more and more the ideal, there is a growing field open to the clever woman who can create sales and will train herself for the real estate field. There are large earnings here for women who can make good, and altho sales may be few and far between, nevertheless there are women who clear $5,000 a year and more in the real estate field, because of well-developed ability, fine personality, and sometimes because of wide social acquaintance.

The insurance field is somewhat similar to the real estate field in its opportunities. There is great competition, but the mere fact that one is a woman is quite an asset in this work, according to the admissions of some successful agents. The man insurance agent has been classed, very often, with the famed "book agent," and receives about the same kind of welcome and encouragement. Women who sell insurance are likely to receive a hearing where men can not. Women, too, are more likely to base their arguments on human appeals, which in this work are often more winning than stereotyped business arguments.

Then there is a field of indirect selling which is opening opportunities to alert women. This is the field for the demonstrator-saleswoman. The jobber of a branded line of distinctive foods may employ for "missionary work" a woman whose official title is "chief demonstrator," and whose work is half advertising and half selling. She travels over the country, visiting dealers, who cooperate with her, by giving her the use of their store to make a "pure-food" display. Sometimes it is accompanied by a daily lecture or a cooking demonstration given by one of the staff of demonstrators whom she recruits in each city she visits. This demonstration may be made for one or more dealers in a town, and, of course, it always results in orders for the "chief demonstrator." Another type of indirect saleswoman is an interior decorator who travels in the interest of a large paint manufacturer. She lectures before women's clubs, gets up special displays of attractive interiors for dealers, featuring particular paints and finishes of the house. While not, strictly speaking, a saleswoman, she is, nevertheless a splendid sales developer.

This sales-demonstration work is the door through which many women may enter the wholesale selling field in an even larger way. Demonstration work is on a much higher level than it was years ago, when it conveyed to the average mind a picture of an ingratiating feminine person who rattled off a mechanical speech about magic hair-restorers or undetectable complexion aids, or never-failed-yet furniture polish. To-day demonstration often means high-class lecture work, and it is the kind of a post that a clever women can create for herself and make valuable. The woman who represents a manufacturer of labor-saving machinery for the home—fireless cookers, or washing machines, or vacuum-cleaners—may be a well-educated woman able to lecture well about home management. Some years ago a high-class New York department store featured for a week the lecturer of a corset manufacturer. In a beautiful auditorium she lectured daily to women on the subject of bodily hygiene, how to adapt a corset to one's individual needs, etc. She created a demand for the corset in that store, and, of course, she booked a good-sized order. The possibilities of the demonstration field in its highest selling sense have not been touched, and certainly it contains opportunities for the woman who has good presence, is able to lecture, and possesses sales ability.

How can an inexperienced woman train for outside salesmanship? What should be her basis of equipment? Can she hope to succeed in this comparatively new profession for women? She can if she will accept two modern opinions. One is the business theory that good salesmen are made by training. Nobody is born either a capable or an inefficient seller of merchandise. The second is the claim of psychologists that it is will and incentive that make for success in any work, not inherited genius or accidental ability. So the woman who desires to sell can equip herself, if she have good health, energy, and sufficient optimism to sustain her during the hard pull upward. Her program might be somewhat as follows:

(1) Plunge into the field at once. Get some outside selling experience, even if it is only six months of selling subscriptions. This will rub off the raw edges of inexperience, and will provide, by daily contact, the elements of selling psychology.

(2) Simultaneously study the theory of selling. There are many excellent books, magazines and courses of study, some of which are mentioned in the bibliography.

(3) Then try to get a post in some organization that maintains a system of training for its field staff.

The practical schooling given in large organizations, plus theoretical study, should provide a fine foundation for successful selling for any ambitious woman. If she keeps on studying the theory of selling, and psychology as applied to selling, in addition to gathering practical experience, she will develop her own principles of selling and equip herself for one of the most constructive, most stimulating and most profitable branches of business occupation.

XV

OPPORTUNITIES IN THE RETAIL AND DEPARTMENT STORES

SELLING merchandise in a retail way is a far more pleasant job than some others, and contains many more opportunities. This is because it involves the handling of beautiful or useful equipment for the home or person, and because it develops a first-hand knowledge of human nature. The saleswoman's chief stock-in-trade is her skilfulness in human contact, and the necessity for exercising her charm and mentality to make each meeting produce good results.

Occasionally we hear that the work is unhygienic. But physicians affirm that if conditions of light, heat and ventilation are good, if provision is made for occasional sitting, if the worker wears sensible garments and low-heeled, comfortable shoes, the work is by no means unwholesome. If department-store selling seems monotonous and ill-paid, it is because its opportunities are neglected and warped, or the conditions in that particular organization are unpleasant, and not because the work itself is inimical to commercial progress and personal welfare.

The charge of low wages is, unfortunately, true to a considerable extent, altho there are many first-class department stores where a minimum wage of $8 prevails, even without coercion from a minimum wage commission, and the number of such stores is growing. Why, then, can not all stores do likewise? Consider first a few facts about the modern department store. There are over 32,000 retail dry goods and department stores in this country, whose total sales are estimated at approximately two billion dollars. About one-quarter of this huge total is divided among the seventy-five department stores in the following large cities:

ESTIMATED YEARLY SALES OF 75 DEPARTMENT STORES IN THE FIVE LARGEST CITIES [1]

New York	$191,000,000
Chicago	131,000,000
Philadelphia	65,000,000
Boston	55,500,000
St. Louis	27,000,000

[1] From Curtis Publishing Company's "*Obiter Dicta.*"

This seems like a tremendously large revenue that offers ample means for high wages and profit-making—until it is weighed with other conditions in department-store management.

(1) It costs the average store between 20 to 30 per cent. to do business—a higher percentage than any other retail store except jewelry.
(2) The C. O. D. and charge account systems diminish both sales and profits considerably.
(3) The practise of delivering all goods, even if the cost of delivery is more than the sum total of the bill, is a large item.
(4) Cut-price sales and profitless competition.
(5) Possible low-producing sales force.

This is not a brief for the department store—simply an outline of the facts offered by employers as an explanation of the low wages paid. We are told time and again that legislation can not compel payment of a just minimum wage to all employees now engaged, as long as the business is so conducted that a slight cut into its profits (such as a more generous wage adjustment) would send it into bankruptcy.

Several activities in recent years have affected the position of the girl in the department store. One is the interest of organized consumers, who, by the weight of their influence as buyers, have encouraged stores to provide more comfortable working conditions. The installation of seats on which girls can rest occasionally, better light and ventilation, and the campaign against basement departments, are all making department-store work more wholesome.

Then, too, the consumer's conscience is slowly awakening to the injustice of abusing the "returned goods" privilege, as will be seen by the following resolution, which was presented by the Consumers' League and adopted by the New York City Federation of Women's Clubs (representing 228 organizations):

"*Whereas,* the Consumers' League has found through a study of shopping methods in New York City that the common practise of returning and exchanging goods has assumed such large proportions that it has become a matter of public concern, because

1. This practise brings hardship to employees through the loss of sales; and

2. This practise, particularly as regards wearing apparel, is not for the best interests of public health;
3. This practise adds materially to the cost of business, which is ultimately borne by the customer; be it, therefore,

"*Resolved,* That the New York City Federation of Women's Clubs indorses and supports the efforts of the Consumers' League in discouraging this irresponsible habit among shoppers.

The Consumers' League found, on investigation, that 30 per cent. of all goods purchased on charge accounts were returned for credit; 20 per cent. of all goods shipped C. O. D. were not accepted; 10 per cent. of all cash purchases were exchanged; every fifth pair of shoes sold had to be sold over again. Customers sometimes return goods they have held for six months, and, as styles shift rapidly, many of these articles are utterly unsalable. It has been the unreasonable demands of women shoppers which have kept the saleswomen down to low wages as much as grasping employers!

Stores of the more progressive type are doing a great deal in the way of educating salespeople to higher efficiency. In New

York, Boston, Philadelphia and other cities the schools and the stores cooperate in educational work for employees, and the expense is borne by the store. Other stores maintain schools and a permanent teaching staff. Especially valuable work is being done in Boston by the Union School of Salesmanship and in New York by the Department Store Educational Association. A significant principle of the latter organization is that, while so many semi-philanthropic organizations have set out with the single motive of raising wages, this Association has tackled the problem from its basis, not from its conclusion. It started with the proposition that the permanent incentive for good work is not only salary, but interest in work. Create interest in the work, and the pay will take care of itself. With this view-point in mind, a rational method of education to interest department-store workers in the job for its own sake was begun. Daily instruction is given to groups of saleswomen in a definite course of study, by experts on the staff of the Association.

RETAIL AND DEPARTMENT STORES

OUTLINE OF COURSE

STOCK—

Classification in department.
Arrangement and care.
Color, form and style.
Materials and qualities—silk, cotton, leather, straw, felt, etc.

SALESMANSHIP—

Types of customers.
Methods of approach.
How to close a sale.
Demonstration sale for discussion.

MERCHANDISING PRINCIPLES—

Quick selling and profits.
Store policies.
Waste.

COMMERCIAL ETHICS—

Relation of employees to store.
Relation of employees to customers.
Relation of employees to each other.

SYSTEM—

Methods of rapid calculation, fractions, discounts, etc.
Business English.
Geography of New York.

This outline of study is a comparatively simple one that can be arranged for any store, large or small. A local library contains volumes on the textiles and commodities that the women handle, and in which they grow tremendously interested, once study is begun. At the end of the course each employee is graded according to her work, so that in addition to educating the employee the course supplies executives with a basis for judging efficiency and determining promotion.

One of the valuable features of this work is that it is preparing the ground for better methods of fixing salaries and promotions. Theoretically, it may seem simple to decide on what is a just salary for a seller of merchandise, because the results are measurable. Indeed, a common statement is that "a saleswoman should be paid about 4 per cent. of her gross sales. A saleswoman should sell about $150 worth of merchandise each week to be paid $6; $300 per week to be paid $12," and so on.

It would be simple to pay saleswomen a blanket percentage of their sales if every saleswoman had an equally advantageous

(No. 9)—RECORD CARD FOR SALESPEOPLE[2]

	Date..........		
	Perfect record	*Actual record*	*Record 1 year later*
PHYSICAL (Total 20 points)—			
(a) Health	10	....	....
(b) Appearance:			
Bearing	2	....	....
Clothes	2	....	....
Cleanliness	2	....	....
(c) Voice	2	....	....
(d) Speech	2	....	....
INTELLECTUAL (Total 27 points)—			
(a) Knowledge of English..........	4	....	....
(b) General education..........	4	....	....
(c) Technical knowledge:			
Knowledge of the house (policies, organization, history, competitors)	4	....	....
Knowledge of the goods..........	7	....	....
Knowledge of people..........	8	....	....
PERSONALITY (Total 23 points)—			
(a) Inclination to business..........	1	....	....
(b) Ambition	2	....	....
(c) Self-confidence	2	....	....
(d) Determination	1	....	....
(e) Honesty	2	....	....
(f) Agreeableness	1	....	....
(g) Courtesy	5	....	....
(h) Purity	1	....	....
(i) Willingness to learn..........	1	....	....
(j) Willingness to cooperate..........	1	....	....
(k) Promptness	1	....	....
(l) Frankness	1	....	....
(m) Imagination	2	....	....
(n) Enthusiasm and love of selling....	2	....	....
SALESMANSHIP—			
(a) Care of stock and department.....	2	....	....
(b) Getting attention..........	3	....	....
(c) Describing and showing goods....	3	....	....
(d) Meeting objections..........	3	....	....
(e) Persistence	5	....	....
(f) Convincing the customer..........	4	....	....
(g) Closing the sale..........	5	....	....
(h) Making customer permanent......	5	....	....
Total..........	100	....	....

[2] From "Retail Selling & Store Management," by Prof. Paul H. Nystrom.

position, equally staple stock—and there were no bargain counters. But there are bargain counters where hard-working girls can sell $200 worth of goods per week without exercising any selling skill—and because these are bargain counters, and there is no profit on the goods, the girls are not paid more than $6 per week. No matter how hard she works, the girl who sells spools of thread and hairpins can not achieve a $500-a-week mark, as the saleswoman in the coats and wraps department can. An equitable standard of wages must take into consideration the nature of the commodity, the accessibility of the department, the special difficulties of selling, and perhaps some more factors, and the wages fixt for individual departments.

In the meantime, a reasonable basis of wages is the saleswoman's record in school work as disclosed by examination, plus a record of her sales, plus her buyer's estimate. Prof. Paul H. Nystrom has prepared a chart for judging salespeople. The buyer or department head or employment manager marks this card annually, or semi-annually, basing his opinion on observation of the individual, record of sales, opinion of the employee's immediate superior. Any one receiving 70 to 80 points is fair; 80 to 90 is good, and above that number, exceptional; to be rewarded accordingly.

There is no doubt that the job of selling to women, interesting as it is, requires a large amount of patience and tact. The average woman who shops, even in the fairest spirit, is nevertheless out to get the most for her money. She wants not only good merchandise, but she wants also information, attention and the best she can get for the smallest expenditures. Sometimes she is a nervous person, uncertain, indecisive, impatient. Then it is necessary to help her make up her mind, in a quiet, tactful way. She must not be argued with—everything she is told must be simply a quiet explanation of facts which suggests a decision. One has to be especially courteous to the irritable customer, as much for the sake of one's own nerves as for the welfare of the house. Sometimes extreme politeness shames the inconsiderate customer into courtesy.

Helpful stock-in-trade for the saleswoman is having novel information about her merchandise. Everything in the world has an interesting story about its origin or production, if only we dig patiently for it in books, encyclopedias, trade papers, etc. Here is a suggested outline for the process of making a sale:

(1) Know something interesting to say about your merchandise. Don't depend on the low price to make the sale. Have some ideas about its use. If you sell food or textiles, you may be able to show how to test it for purity, or explain how tests may be made. Try to interest your customer and her mind will be opened to suggestion and conviction.

(2) Watch the facial expressions of your customer when she talks, and adjust your talk accordingly. Do your utmost to keep her in a pleasant frame of mind. A cross or displeased person never makes a favorable decision.

(3) Tell your story quickly and simply. Answer questions briefly, but completely and courteously. Talk quality, or use, or saving of time or labor, according to the nature of your stock. Never concentrate on price; because, if the price is high, the customer will hesitate about buying; and if it

is low, she is likely to be offended if classed with bargain-hunters.

(4) As soon as there is a pause, suggest a decision. Don't say, "Will you take this?" but ask her whether she will have it sent or take it with her; or how much of it she wants. If she has been kept in a pleasant attitude, your inference that she will buy will help her make up her mind more quickly.

Some time ago a New York newspaper raised the question, "Why are women not employed behind the silk counter?" It called forth many replies from department-store authorities, which, summarized, amount to this:

(1) Women do not know enough about silk to answer questions intelligently.

(2) They do not know how to fold silk properly; they fold it carelessly so that the fabric is injured and must be sold at a reduction.

(3) Silk sales run into large sums, and women shoppers look upon it as an important purchase. Hence they prefer the services of the earnest salesman who tries his best to make a sale, rather than the services of a

girl, who so often acts as tho she were perfectly indifferent as to whether the customer bought or not.

Other reasons were suggested, but the thought-provoking criticism is the first reason advanced—that women do not know silk. It is a curious fact that, while women easily keep up-to-the-minute information on fashions, which are constantly changing, they know very few of the permanent facts about textiles which would enable them to buy more intelligently. The average shopper does not know textiles at all. Consequently, the well-informed saleswoman who can tell her how to select the pure silk from the weighted silk; how to detect all wool from part shoddy, and so on, enlists her confidence and influences sales. The teaching of facts about textiles and manufacturing processes is one of the first and most important branches of department-store educational work. But the alert saleswoman can follow up the beginnings of her store education. There is a wealth of information available in every public library, which will make her not only a more efficient saleswoman, but will make her work vastly more enjoyable.

The woman who sells apparel successfully is not only a shrewd saleswoman, but a student of form and color—even if she has to take a course in the evenings to get the information she needs. She knows what are good lines and good shades, and she knows how to suggest tactfully the style and color that "bring out the lovely shades of your hair," or "show your lovely figure to best advantage"—not, as a diligent but tactless saleswoman suggested, "what you *ought* to wear." No woman likes to be told what she "ought" to wear, believing herself a competent authority on the subject. The clever saleswoman can use color charts to show what are the best colors for various complexions and facial contours, and form charts to show the lines that should be used to clothe various figures to best advantage.

The successful saleswoman in the furnishings department has a well-developed esthetic sense. She can suggest attractive color schemes, or the right kind of frame for a picture that is to be hung on a wall of a certain tint, or how tables and chairs should be placed. Some of the large department stores offer the services of a trained interior decorator to help select and arrange furnishings artistically. That interior decorator is simply a first-class salesperson with an esthetic sense.

Even in the house-furnishing department—stuck away down in the basement, as it so often is!—there is opportunity for the thinking woman to distinguish herself. So few saleswomen know the uses of the devices they sell. But the saleswoman who shows you how to use labor-saving devices; who can show you how work is made easier, and how much time you can save, and just why it pays to buy a device is a rare treasure. All this information can be gained from books, trade journals and manufacturers' catalogs, at little or no cost, and it adds immeasurably to the saleswoman's assets. The only way the saleswoman can equip herself for a bigger job is by education.

TEN COMMANDMENTS FOR A RETAIL MERCHANT [3]

1. Confine purchases to as few houses as possible.
2. Do not overbuy.
3. Take all discounts and pay all bills when due.
4. Have some books, especially an accurate ex-

[3] From "The Monthly Bulletin" of the National Association of Credit Men, New York.

pense account, a daily sales record, a book showing purchases, with cost, and when due.

5. Carry enough insurance.
6. Make accurate reports to the commercial agencies.
7. Keep a clean, well-arranged store.
8. Do as much cash business as possible.
9. Do not make unjust claims.
10. Live within your means.

Selling ability is a weapon which makes a woman self-sufficient and independent, because business is always willing to give an opportunity to the woman who is able to make sales. There is competition for the services of the good saleswoman. In some of the New York shops selling high-priced apparel for women expert saleswomen are paid as high as $50 or $60 a week. But there are other opportunities open to the expert seller. The goal of most ambitious young saleswomen is to become one of the fabulously salaried "buyers" who go abroad two or three times a year. Incidentally, one wonders why these foreign business trips of buyers are considered the great attraction of the job. If the whole truth were told, there is often more labor and nervous energy spent in these trips than the amount of pleasure they afford. The job of "buyer" is taxing to the limit in its demands on physical and nervous energy, so the woman who has this ambition must possess, first of all, a sound body and good nervous system. She also must be exceedingly well informed about her stock—the values of competitive merchandise, and selling methods, because the "buyer" is, in reality, a first-class seller. Responsibility for her department rests on her shoulders alone. And so she must possess a keen scent for what the public might want, knowledge to buy well, so that she can sell at a profit, and ability to attract customers. She is literally the manager of a store, for she is "charged" with the cost of running her department—the advertising, the display and salaries. Her job depends on how much profit she is able to produce by her management and buying.

The buyer's job is one of the biggest in business, requiring as it does, a fine grasp of things, knowledge of selling, knowledge of commodities, and administrative ability. It is a stimulating goal for any business woman. But the number of places as buyers is so rare, compared to the number of aspirants, that we must look to another field for the reward of efficient salesmanship.

The big, unlimited, most desirable field for the abilities of the woman who can sell is a business of her own. The saleswoman who can not obtain as high a price for her services as she considers them worth, the woman who has had buying experience, or who has been assistant to a buyer, has an excellent foundation for succeeding in a shop of her own. In New York City there are hundreds of "specialty shops" along Fifth Avenue and elsewhere for the exclusive sale of one or two kinds of articles, like gowns, gloves, hats, corsets, etc., the proprietors of which are women, most of them with department store experience. But the woman with business proprietorship as her goal begins long beforehand to equip herself with the knowledge necessary for retail business administration. She knows more than the details of her own job. She studies the details of store management; the art of display in the store; window trims that are attractive; arrangement of departments and the featuring of certain goods so as to influence sales.

An important branch of information so often neglected by saleswomen because it is not part of their immediate needs, is the ideals of store policy. The modern store is past the old maxim, *caveat emptor,* "let the buyer beware." As one department-store manager announced to new employees, "The boss of this store is the customer." And so the policy of price-fixing, making of comparative prices, how to meet competition, the making of adjustments, must be established with due regard to the requirements of the public, and the margin of profit which the business allows. How shall the proper margin of profit be determined? The successful woman merchandiser knows all about the possible leaks in a retail business—like theft, fire, over-measurement, poor care of merchandise, poor packing, waste supplies, unsalable stock, waste light, goods lost in transit, clerk's errors, employees' waste of time, goods so poorly sold that there is a loss of good will. She knows how to anticipate and prevent many of them.

The woman preparing for business ownership also begins early to adopt the "employer" rather than the "employee" view-point. The woman with the "employee" view-point is content to stick to her one little round of duties. She closes her mind to anything outside. "Oh, that kind of information is for the buyer, or for the manager. I don't have to know it." She "waits" for promotion, and her chief ambition in life is to get a raise. The woman with the "employer view-point" visualizes herself as an employer, rather than a subordinate worker. She fills her mind with the interests that occupy an employer—ideas about improving service, not only as far as it affects her immediate work, but as it affects her department and the entire business. Nothing that has any relation to her business, no matter how remote, passes her by. She searches for facts, reads, takes courses, clips from periodicals anything that relates to her business.

The saleswoman with executive ambitions knows not only her own job, but commodities, and business administration. While she is still an employee she studies employees' attitude toward work; how they can be inspired to produce more for themselves and for the business, what schooling they need, and what stimulation and compensation methods. What are the best ways of safeguarding their health and physical comfort —ventilation, heating systems, rest periods, vacations, etc. No detail is too small to escape her for future use. Consequently, she is not only an able saleswoman, but has a more sympathetic insight into the difficulties of store management, and her manner of effort is, therefore, likely to win her favorable recognition, even if she remains an employee for a long time. Not every saleswoman will realize her ambition for store ownership; but every saleswoman who prepares herself to own a business will be a better saleswoman because she works with that aim in mind.

XVI

WOMEN AS BUSINESS EXECUTIVES

WHY is a woman president of a business so rare that, as soon as she is discovered she is interviewed to tell an eager public how she accomplished the miracle? Any woman who manages a business, even if it be only a muffin bakery in her home kitchen, inspires more talk and congratulation than the man who owns a railroad. Only one out of every 80 women in business can be counted in the executive class, if we accept census figures. There were approximately four times as many men as women in paid occupations in 1910, yet there were fifteen times as many men as women executives. To put it differently, 94 per cent. of all the executive jobs were held by men, and only 6 per cent. by women. This seems to indicate quite definitely that women are the serving class in business. One reason for this extraordinary difference in the proportion of women executives to the total number of women at work is that one-quarter of the total were in personal or domestic service which is not considered executive work, because it is usually supervised by the unpaid home-maker.

What, then, is an executive position? It may be defined as a post involving supervision of others, or responsibility for initiating or managing an enterprise. An owner or official in a corporation, like president, secretary, treasurer, is an executive because she carries responsibility for the management of the enterprise. A superintendent, manager or forewoman is an executive because she must supervise others. An executive is either the proprietor or one of the governing or departmental heads of a business.

In conducting retail establishments, women have distinguished themselves as executives, and there is one woman to every 16 men who own retail stores. Another occupation in which women have proved good executives is in the management of hotels and restaurants, for there is one woman to every 4 men managing such places.

But in practically every other executive

post of importance, women are very poorly represented. The number of women who own or manage manufacturing establishments is amazingly small. Yet, does it not seem logical to suppose that, if women followed home industries out of the home into the factory (as has been repeated hundreds of times) that women would initiate and manage the enterprises that manufacture home products? Who is it that to-day own the large nationally famous manufacturies that produce textiles and apparel and soap and canned soup and bread and candy? Men mostly. There is but one woman manufacturer to every 53 men manufacturers.

In financial matters, too, woman, the traditionally great conserver, has trailed considerably behind men. There are very few women bankers or brokers or officials in transportation enterprises where financial ability is a prerequisite. Here is a detailed statement of the position of women to-day in their relation to the executive opportunities of business, taken from a statistical abstract published by the United States government—P. 229—1913 ed.:

WOMEN AS BUSINESS EXECUTIVES

MEN AND WOMEN HOLDING EXECUTIVE POSITIONS

TRADE:	*Men*	*Women*
Retail proprietors	1,127,926	67,103
Bankers, and bank officials, brokers and commission	103,170	2,634
Floorwalkers and foremen	17,649	3,075
Officials of insurance companies	9,376	125
Other proprietors and managers	21,352	1,010
Total executives in trade	1,279,473	73,947

Number of men in trade................ 4,290,411

Number of women in trade............. 1,061,312

MANUFACTURING AND MECHANICAL INDUSTRIES:	*Men*	*Women*
Proprietors and officials	251,892	4,699
Managers and superintendents	102,748	1,462
Foremen, forewomen, overseers	155,358	19,740
Total executives in manufacturing	509,998	25,901

Number of men in manufacturing and mechanical 8,837,901

Number of women in manufacturing and mechanical 1,820,980

TRANSPORTATION:	*Men*	*Women*
Proprietors and officials of telegraph and telephone companies	8,680	1,409
Proprietors of other transportation	4,731	19
Officials and superintendents of steam and street railroad companies	22,236	2
Foremen and overseers in railroad transportation	69,693	240
Proprietors and managers of transfer and livery	50,980	413
Total executives in transportation	156,320	2,083

Number of men in transportation........ 2,531,075

Number of women in transportation...... 106,596

DOMESTIC AND PERSONAL SERVICE:

	Men	Women
Hotel-keepers and managers......	50,269	14,235
Restaurant, cafe and lunch-room keepers	50,316	10,516
Laundry owners and managers....	17,057	986
Total executives in domestic and personal service	117,642	25,737
Number of men in domestic and personal service	1,241,238	
Number of women in domestic and personal service	2,530,846[1]	

PUBLIC SERVICE:

	Men	Women
Officials and inspectors (city).....	32,199	1,011
Officials and inspectors (county)..	17,469	1,575
Officials and inspectors (state)....	6,662	540
Officials and inspectors (federal).	36,727	8,997
Total executives in public service	93,057	11,123
Number of men in public service.........	445,733	
Number of women in public service......	13,558	

SUMMARY:

	Men	Women
Total number in all occupations (including occupations not listed in above groups)	37,027,558	8,075,772
Number of executives	2,156,490	138,791

When we ask why so comparatively small a proportion of women workers are executives, we are offered several explanations:

[1] Unfortunately, this figure includes both paid housekeepers and the married women, who are unpaid home-makers, due to the failure of many of the census-takers to distinguish between the two.

(1) Women do not remain in industry long enough to become executives; (2) Men have a prejudice against women executives; (3) Women lack preparation for business proprietorship, or executive posts; they dislike responsibility.

The first explanation is in line with the popular theory that women always marry, and when they marry they leave industry permanently. In that case, we should find only young women in industry, but facts are otherwise. Out of every 100 men at work 83 are over 21 years of age, 26 are over 45 years of age. Out of every 100 women at work 68 are over 21 years of age and 15 are over 45 years of age.[2] You see by these figures that after all, there is not such an alarming difference between the proportion of men and proportion of women who are in business at middle age—31 per cent. of men and 22 per cent. of women. In other words, we can assume that out of the 8 million women who began a business career, over 1 million have remained in or turned to business by the time they reach the age of 45. Therefore the first argument that a

[2] *Bulletin on Occupation Statistics,* 13th Census, pp. 45-46.

sufficiently large proportion of women do not remain in industry long enough to become executives can not be true.

The second argument—that men object to a woman executive—is only a half-truth. There still are men who will quote historical and biological authorities to prove that a woman can not be an executive. They tell us that woman is not naturally dynamic—that her race history and physiological make-up equip her only for static functions as a conserver, not as an aggressive developer like men. They tell us that a woman has not the courage to take big risks in commercial enterprises, as a man does; that a woman's courage is spasmodic and usually an emotional reaction, not an everyday habit as it must be to a man with executive responsibilities. And when we speak of a Hetty Green or Mrs. Sage in refutation, we are told that women financiers of this type did not create their wealth by courageous endeavor, but simply conserved an inherited capital. Even our proud references to some distinctively successful women manufacturers of clothes and candy and biscuits are dismissed by a comparison to the vastly superior success of the bread and candy and clothing corporations floated and managed by men. This is a summary of some typical opinions of men who are prejudiced against women as executives.

On the other hand, there is a growing percentage of men who are willing and eager to cooperate with women in executive work. There are good reasons. Eventually most of all the products manufactured and distributed are bought by women, either for the home or for the individuals of a home. Women know better than men what women want to buy and what the home needs. And so, even if men are manufacturers or head large distributing enterprises, they recognize the great value of the woman's viewpoint in business. Indeed, if there were more women executives in manufactories, there would undoubtedly be less of the inefficient, unpractical, undesirable commodities for the home dumped on the market. And so many women who occupy important executive posts to-day gladly admit that their upward climb has been aided vastly by the cooperation and counsel of business men. The opposition from some men is not an insurmountable obstacle to the able women, trained and ambitious for executive responsibility. More than anything else, lack of preparation and lack of desire for a high commercial goal has kept women from executive posts.

Sometimes a very able woman is entirely content with one of the secondary executive positions with which business abounds. Every department of the large modern organization requires an executive who is a "detail executive." There must be a responsible individual to operate smoothly the departments of accounting, credit, correspondence, mailing, order, shipping and stenographic work. Each of these departments is honeycombed with intricate detail requiring the supervision of a conscientious martinet. Observe that these departments require attention to things—actual orders or letters, concrete matter to be checked or counted. You rarely find a woman in charge of a department of ideas like the advertising or sales department where creativeness and abstract thinking are required.

All these minor executive posts—manager of a billing department, or stenographic department, etc.,—give excellent training to a woman. Women are usually found more efficient and conscientious in these jobs. But, it must not be assumed that a managing job as a detail executive is the limit of a woman's executive capacity. To the woman with high ideals about her own ability, this is simply a stepping-stone to bigger things, exactly as it would be to a man. Such an appointment should be recognized as a signal to begin training for broader executive management, with due consideration for this peculiar condition.

Very often promotion to an executive position is given not as a recognition of executive ability, but as a species of reward for long and satisfactory service in subordinate work. It is assumed that if Miss Jones could be so excellent a bill clerk for so many years, she is amply qualified to manage the billing department. If she turns out to be only a mediocre manager, she wonders why; but the reason is not far to seek. She knows nothing about management of her department, and to be a good manager requires other abilities than to be a good detail worker. Efficiency in operation and efficiency in management are two widely different abilities. A knowledge of mathematics and dexterity with the typewriter might be quite sufficient equipment for a first-class bill clerk. But the best type of manager for the billing department has a working knowledge of the entire business, so that the billing department can cooperate as a helpful unit. Also the post requires definite ability and information in the science of management so that there may be intelligent and sympathetic relations with employees.

A common and disastrous experience of many sales organizations has come from promoting the most successful road salesman to the sales-managership. It has been proved often that the man who can sell goods is the least able to manage the men who sell goods. It is because there is so wide a difference between the knowledge of how to work and the knowledge of managing men who do the work. There are many eminently successful sales-managers who never sell a dollar's worth of goods themselves. But they know how to build and stimulate a sales organization that produces splendid results. It is because they are essentially large-plan, not detail individuals. They are like generals on a battlefield, expert in the strategy of attack, and the selecting and managing of men to carry out details of instruction.

Consequently, the woman with executive ambitions begins early to study the science of management, so that she is guarded against failure when her opportunity arrives. In analyzing the reasons why only 60,000 of the 250,000 corporations in this country earn more than $5,000 a year and 100,000 make nothing at all, Edward N. Hurley, Vice-president of the Federal Trade Commission declared that "What business needs to-day is—better methods."

It is only by training for executive management that the business woman is able to operate better methods that insure success. It is only by studying the experience of others, by knowing the principles of business as they apply to finance, distribution, and the building of an efficient organization that the pitfalls of business can be avoided. Consequently, she supplements her own practical experience in store or office or factory by definite education in the science of management, as it is offered in institutions or special courses. Simply defined, "scientific management" is the name of a group of business principles which, when applied correctly, produce the maximum results with the minimum of human effort and waste. It is too large a subject to be discust in this chapter, but a list of authoritative works on the subject is appended. Always scientific management includes Ideals, Study of Separate Tasks, and Standardizing Efficient Methods of Performance; the Fair Deal to Workers; and Principles of Authority Distribution.

Many women have the superficial impression that "Scientific Management" is something that is useful in the factory or to railroads, because they have heard so much of scientific management only in connection with those fields. Echoes of the work of Taylor, Harrington Emerson, Frank Gilbreth and other pioneers come to them. We have heard how Harrington Emerson, by applying his twelve principles of efficiency, standardized the Santa Fé Railroad and saved millions of dollars for it, simultaneously providing better service for the public and better conditions for their employees. Frank

Gilbreth, with his motion studies, changed methods of bricklaying, that had been followed for a thousand years, so that to-day men do not have to spend half their time stooping and carrying, but their equipment is scientifically grouped near, and when they work they work laying bricks, not in unnecessary stooping and carrying.

But these motion studies and standardization of tasks and working conditions are being applied to all fields—store, office and even in the home. No one can manage a business properly who does not know the principles of business administration—equipment, distribution of work, management of employees; and so the best foundation for a future of executive responsibility is an adequate grasp of the subject of scientific management in its many phases.

Being a successful executive requires long and arduous training, with heavy responsibility as the reward, and many women ask, with reason, if it is necessary and worth while. Signs of the time point to this fact: More and more, responsibility for self-support is voluntarily adopted, or involuntarily thrust on the modern woman. If she rests content in her economic independence in some subordinate, comfortable job, the day may come when she will "grow rusty," and will be supplanted by younger or cheaper or better help. There are thousands of women to whom just this thing has happened. They have occupied a certain post for years, content, unaspiring, in a pleasant rut. At 35 or 40, filled with the ineradicable habits incident to one type of job, they lose that position. They rarely or never get such another post, and eventually are glad to accept work at any pittance. The business woman of fifty, suddenly thrust out of a subordinate job, may be in the prime of intelligence, but too often she has the difficult task of making her services wanted by the business man who seeks new, fresh ideas, and the virility of youth.

The best safeguard of a woman against a business man's prejudice toward the apparently superannuated is—her own business, begun early. It is far better to operate one's own business, no matter how small, than to be even an important subordinate in a large organization. A business of your own calls forth every latent energy and ability; it develops the creative faculty and arouses the aggressive, constructive spirit that strengthens character against the vicissitudes of life. The woman who bears the brunt of her own business is not "thin-skinned" and hypersensitive. She learns how to face difficulties.

Of course, it is possible to share in the responsibilities of a business even if one is not an owner. But so rarely do women who hold big executive jobs in an organization realize the wisdom of investing in the business they serve. Many organizations encourage investment by employees because of the psychological effect. The attitude changes from that of the employee who wants to get as much as possible out of the business to that of the partial proprietor who will exercise all her faculties to increase business success. It must not be understood that investment in the business is a security against dismissal—and this is its disadvantage as compared with the proprietorship of a business. But the woman holding a big executive post who invests some of her own money in the company she serves has the comforting assurance that even if she loses her job she will continue to share in some measure in the success she has helped to create.

Executive work means training, study, great responsibility. But if women are to stay in business they will either shoulder this responsibility and compete with men on a basis of unqualified efficiency—or they will face the fact that they are a serving class in business and remain in a serving class open-eyed, minus any agitation about equal pay for equal work. The progress of women in business thus far makes the latter contingency altogether unlikely. We are in business to stay. We are unwilling to stay in a rut, even a comfortable rut—and speculate fearfully about the future. We shall prepare to be business executives just as men prepare.

XVII

SPECIAL MISSIONS; COMMERCIALIZING NON-COMMERCIAL OCCUPATIONS

SUPPOSING you are unequipped or have a reasonable distaste for standard lines of business, and yet face the need and desire to earn your own livelihood. There are two courses open. One is to endeavor to create some "special mission" in business; the other to help in the pioneer work of commercializing some of the non-commercial occupations. The peculiar needs of business make it necessary occasionally to find a woman possessing certain gifts—not necessarily commercial altogether—to assume unusual responsibilities. The following description of a few posts falling into this class may suggest other possible avenues of employment that your special abilities may open to you:

A librarian with a special taste for research work decided to enter business, and created for herself an interesting post as "business librarian" in a large corporation. It was her task to read all the printed matter she could find pertaining to the industry. She clipt from newspapers and magazines; she kept in touch with publishers so that she would know all the books new and old that related to her work; she read and clipt from technical and trade papers; she visited manufactories and exhibitions and made notes of new facts; she prepared reports, classified and filed her information so that it was available to any one in the organization who happened to be interested. What was more, she made it her business to bring special articles of value to the attention of department managers who might benefit by the information it contained. Eventually she built a splendid individual library for the organization which saved it time, labor and large sums in the information so intelligently sifted and collected.

Increasing desire for statistical data which is the basis of modern business, is opening several special missions for women of education and intelligencce. This need for better data has led to the professionalizing of that most neglected of office jobs—filing—and as has been explained in a previous chapter, the intelligent woman can develop a filing job into the more important post of business librarian.

Business investigation is another type of special mission. The business investigator possesses some reportorial ability, and she is in demand by large corporations, advertisers and magazines. For example, one clever woman investigator was paid a large sum by a certain advertiser to find out what make of automobile was used by each member of a wealthy club. Another woman investigator was employed by a hardware manufacturer to interview architects. Another worked with a large staff calling on householders for data. The work is difficult; it requires tact, resourcefulness, persistence and an agreeable personality. But it is one of the jobs in which women seem to be more successful than men simply because they are women. A woman is received courteously where a man would be denied an audience. Moreover, the feminine conversational arts are here employed with prodigious success. The individual interviewed is questioned on his particular affairs, and what man was ever unwilling to discourse about himself when skilfully led on by a woman?

It is not necessary that the woman investigator should be a good writer, as the woman reporter must be. Some of the best women investigators are simply ingenious and persistent women who go after facts and get facts. The sums paid for this work vary. Sometimes the work brings a salary of $20 or $30 weekly; sometimes more. Occasionally a contract may be given to the woman investigator which runs into several hundred dollars, and her profit will depend on the quickness and economy with which she can obtain the information.

A unique post filled by a woman of rare good judgment and some previous business experience is that of stockholders' representative in a large corporation. Her status is neither secret nor disguised. All the facts of the business are available to her at all times. She can ask and receive from any official of the company any piece of information she wishes. She keeps careful record of conditions, and renders regular reports to stockholders. Her salary is paid by the stockholders, and she holds her position not only because the stockholders want some one to guard their interests, but because the officials of the company desire to keep stockholders fully informed of the affairs of the company.

In factories, department stores, and organizations employing large numbers of men and women, the "welfare secretary" holds an important position. Usually she is a mature woman of education; sometimes a woman who has taught school or been in contact with large numbers of girls. Her task is to keep in close touch with all the girls, to listen to their woes sometimes; but largely to awaken them to greater interest in their own welfare—to stimulate them into seeking more education, wider reading, to form clubs for self-development and entertainment. Sometimes she acts as a sort of buffer between the management and the workers, for it is inevitable that even in the best-managed organizations there are employees with the ineradicable class-consciousness that makes them suspicious. On the slightest provocation they are ready to regard the organization as personified Capital the primary object of which is to take advantage of the poor employee. The task of the welfare secretary is to sift the real from the fancied complaint and to see that justice is recognized.

Occasionally the welfare secretary in a large manufacturing plant may be expected to visit workmen's homes, to confer with wives, and give counsel in bettering living conditions. Such a welfare secretary is a mature woman, with home-making experience and a knowledge of dietetics.

Every now and then there crops up a curious mania for glorifying women who enter all sorts of fearful and wonderful occupations formerly monopolized by men —not because the work is desirable, but because women are pioneering in men's fields. To-day there are women "bell-hops," women barbers, women cemetery-keepers and scissor-grinders and even longshoremen. A woman blacksmith or woman lighthousekeeper is good for a story in a periodical any day, not because she is an exceptionally expert worker, but simply because she is doing what is commonly supposed to be a man's work. Now it is not important that women should attempt to enter every field that men have entered, even when it is unprofitable work. Indeed, it is often a calamity.

The fact that a woman somewhere has turned blacksmith is a curious fact of interest, but it does not indicate that blacksmithing is a desirable profession for women, worthy of difficult pioneering work. The truth is that the publicity given to instances of such odd careers for women has injured more than helped the industrial position of women. It has spread an impression that women were in business because of the spectacular effect they could produce, and that their interest in business was not serious, but of a hectic, evanescent character. Everything that tends to draw sharp sex-contrasts between men and women in industry emphasizes the need for discriminating between men and women in industrial opportunity and remuneration. That is the danger that confronts all women when a few women engage in freak occupations.

The woman with some business ability and a taste for pioneering work could do nothing better than help in the task of commercializing the tasks of home—helping to put the average home on a more business-like basis. The whole problem of home-making to-day could be solved by the application of business principles. But the average home-maker knows nothing about business, and admits much more frequently than the man who supports that home, that her work is too much for her. The average home-maker has not received the training to plan her work, nor how to select tools, nor how to manage her employees. It is to the everlasting glory of a small minority of home-makers that they persistently fight their handicaps, but it is too often at the expense of personal health, and the sacrifice of larger interests, because there has been no time in which to pursue such interests.

It will be the task of business women to plunge into the problem and help solve it. Business women are trained to plan work so that the tasks of each day are finished. A chronic wail from the homemaker is, "Why can't I secure an assistant in the home who will help me as much as my husband's assistant helps him in his office?" The business woman should logically be able to formulate the schedules, hours of work and methods of compensation that will make housework a desirable profession, attracting intelligent types of women.

From many view-points, the home is a highly desirable field of professionalized occupation for women. It is the one occupation that is busy the year 'round and never has an off season. War or peace, we must all eat, wear clean linen, and live in a cared-for house every single day. Somebody must do these things, and few are doing them well. Domestic help is inadequate, competent household workers are very rare, and the expert cook or home manager is coming to be a luxury only for the idle rich. Indeed, we may see the day when men will recognize the possibilities of the work that never has a dull season, and will undertake the management of homes on a commercial basis, employing women as subordinates in women's own job—unless we intervene in time! Men have already established the commercial laundry; the commercial cleaning systems, and the delicatessen shop is gradually encroaching on the domain of the home kitchen.

There are thousands of girls in business who hate their typewriters, but love to keep house, and are yearning for the day when marriage will give them the opportunity of doing the preferred work. There are thousands of homes in which the work of such women would be highly appreciated, and well paid. Even now housework is better paid than many subordinate posts in business. The stenographer at $12 a week, with her board and carfare to pay out of that sum, may have about 10 per cent. of her salary saved, if she is economical; but the houseworker at $25 a month and no board or carfare to pay can have about 60 per cent. of her salary saved. The disadvantages in housework are its irregular hours, unstandardized compensation, the social stigma which attaches to the work, because the employee lives in the home she serves, is more or less under surveillance and has little personal liberty. And so there seems a permanent hiatus between the girl who would rather do housework than any other work, and the home that needs her. There is a movement afoot to educate public opinion to the point where fallacious and snobbish prejudices against the houseworker as distinguished from the factory worker or office worker will disappear. There are many authorities who believe that the prejudice of well-educated women against housework will be overcome with more business-like hours in the home, better tools and equipment, better planning, and last, but not least, by a standard of remuneration which will make it possible for the household employee to live in her own home just as does the business employee.

There are many excellent schools of training in the domestic occupations and they prepare for interesting and remunerative work in many branches outside of teaching the subjects so learned. Following is given a list of some standard, and some new home occupations that are available to the trained woman:

	Approximate average wage *Monthly*
Cook and housekeeper......	$35.00 and maintenance
Managing housekeeper	30.00 " "
Matron of institution.......	45.00 " "
Dieticians..................	100.00 and residence
House mother	75.00 " "
Manager of lunchroom.....	100.00
Household counselor and home efficiency engineer	(Varying fees)

There is great need for dietetic information, especially by middle-class women who can afford only a small price for the service. The very poor get excellent free counsel from local settlement workers; the rich have their own specialists; but the great middle class, the business woman's own class, needs this help. The middle class home-maker rarely receives dietetic training before the responsibilities of home management are upon her. When there are sufficient women in this occupation so that they create a demand for paying service of this kind, and can make their fees moderate, it may be no more uncommon for middle class women to have a "family dietician" to prescribe foods for growing children, planning meals on a small income, etc., than it is now to have a family physician—but the latter's services will be needed less often.

Business corporations that are in out-of-the-way districts very often have a lunch room on the premises. Here is where a business woman dietician is needed to plan the right kind of food for workers. Women's clubs and organizations for business women require the dietician's services. The dietician may later on develop into some line of business occupation, such as manufacturing specially pure foodstuffs, or operating a tea-room, restaurant or even hotel. The women-managed tea-rooms in New York succeed very well, and altho some of them are not most efficiently managed, from the standpoint of service and their charges, nevertheless they are preferred because of the purity of the food and the individual charm of their appointments, which are often much superior to the very good hotels.

Another field for the woman who makes a business of the home is that of counselor in home efficiency. There are at present very few women doing this work, partly because there is still much analysis and investigation to be made to put the ancient industry of the home on a business-like basis; also, because the average home-maker has not been educated to pay a fitting fee for such counsel. There is much pioneer work to be done here. But there is no doubt of its need. The home-maker of moderate means requires expert advice on better arrangement of her kitchen—how to choose home machinery and tools without wasteful experimentation—how to plan her daily work—how to keep business-like record of home expenditures—how to manage household employees.

Since the passage of the Smith-Lever law, a demand has arisen for experienced housekeepers of mature years who can travel into country districts, bringing to the country home-maker information and help about better methods of housekeeping. The Federal Government has made an appropriation for this purpose, which is supplemented by an appropriation by each State. It is said there is more demand for these "field agents" or "home advisers" at present than women to fill vacancies, because the work requires in addition to practical housekeeping experience, some technical training, and also information about up-to-date methods of housekeeping, dietetics, sanitation, account-keeping, etc. This is all typically women's work, and there is no reason why the intelligent business woman can not commercialize home-making tastes and help put this much-maligned industry on a basis where it will attract young women to embark in the business.

Women have always been in the business of agriculture, more or less, but, just like housekeeping, they have not been employed on a business basis. "Back-to-the-land" enthusiasts are urging that a farm of your own is not only an excellent business for self-support, but also is the surest safeguard against an inpecunious old age. Farming to-day is not the haphazard, entirely drudgerous occupation of former years. The modern farm has as much as, and probably more, equipment than the modern office. It is operated on the same principles as a business, with well-standardized machinery for manufacturing, selling, and as great a need for ability in executive management. Like high-type business, farm work too requires training, and the agricultural schools of to-day have a curriculum that is far more adequate and superior to the curriculum of the average business school. The agricultural schools teach students the elements of their profession so that they are efficient under favorable conditions, and they are prepared to combat with the realities of their work.

The Government does a great deal more for workers in farm occupations than in any other line of work. There is more education available, more cooperation, and more supervision. There are county agents who assist the farmers with information; there are granges, State agricultural schools encourage farmers' conventions, and every stimulus is given to greater progress and more education. It may be that in agricultural work the business woman can achieve greater success than in any subordinate post in commercial fields. But it requires training, study, concentration and excellent selling and executive ability—as much as would be required in any manufacturing enterprise.

Mrs. Haviland Lund, founder of the Forward-to-the-Land movement is doing pioneer work, establishing colonies of men and women who decide that they prefer the independence of agriculture to any other form of livelihood.

As a final word it should be said that success is not an accident. Those who fail to win it should not envy the "luck" of those who do.

None is so loud voiced in criticism of "efficiency" as the inefficient. None is so contemptuous of a new method as the individual who has never tried it. None is so positive that it takes no brains to fill a certain position as the individual who has lost an appointment to that job.

On every side we hear that new schemes are "just fads" or "experiments." But whenever we make inquiries we are likely to find that the criticism proceeds more from envy or malice than from a basically sound conception of the object or method criticized. Failures are the most solemn critics of successes. They know it was by some fluke of luck that Harriman became president of some railroad lines. It was just luck or accident or "he hit the psychological moment!"

Of course, it happens occasionally that plums fall into the lap of the undeserving or the effortless. A sawdust-brained youth may inherit a big business from a relative; or a huge fortune with which he can play. Or, a turn of the stock market may reward the speculator far beyond his risk. But no substantial business is built on luck or flourishes on psychological moments. The success developed from the principles of efficiency does not come by accident. Efficiency in its best sense stands for doing the right thing in the right way with the best results and the least expenditure of effort. Then substantial success follows.

APPENDIX

A BIBLIOGRAPHY OF BUSINESS BOOKS, COURSES, AND REFERENCES

"WOMEN don't read business books," is a frequent comment among men. It is true that very often the young business woman at the beginning of her career dismisses from her attention books that relate to business. This is either because she has not been in business long enough to be "commercially curious" and to want to pursue information, or it is because she believes the information "too advanced"; that these business books or courses are for men—the managers and executives.

The most helpful habit that any business woman can form is the habit of assimilating business information of every kind, wherever and whenever she can get it. She should not wait until the day when she will need it. She can be sure that everything she studies about business, about finance, administration, and all specialized data about an industry, will be useful some day, even if it is unrelated to her present work. She should get the habit of reading business books now, and when a bigger opportunity arises, she will be equipped at least with theoretical knowledge which will give her some self-confidence. The following list contains authoritative books which will aid the woman desiring to pursue a special course, or will provide her with information about the opportunities of a particular kind of work:

ON CHOOSING AN OCCUPATION

"Vocations for Girls," E. W. Weaver.

"Vocational Psychology," H. L. Hollingworth (Columbia Univ.).

"Vocations for the Trained Woman," A. F. Perkins (Woman's Industrial & Educational Union).

"How to Get a Position and Keep It," S. Roland Hall.

"American Business Woman," J. M. Crowell.

"The Man, the Job, the Boss," Dr. Katherine M. F. Blackford.

Bulletin No. 14 (Whole No. 587), "Vocational Guidance," U. S. Bureau of Education.

"Vocational Education in Europe," E. C. Cooley.

ON PERSONAL EFFICIENCY AND INSPIRATION

"The Education of Self," Dr. Paul Dubois.

"Increasing Human Efficiency in Business," Prof. Walter Dill Scott.

BIBLIOGRAPHY OF BUSINESS BOOKS

"Essential Elements of Business Character," Herbert V. Stockwell.

"Business Success," Walter Cottingham.

"Business Psychology," Hugo Muensterberg.

"Mental Traits of Sex," H. B. Thompson.

"The Great Society," C. Wallas.

"Manual of Mental and Physical Tests," G. M. Whipple.

"Starting in Life," Nathaniel C. Fowler.

"Imagination in Business," Lorin F. Deland.

"Ready Money," George H. Knox.

"Straight Talks on Business," William Gamble.

"Effective Speaking," A. E. Phillips.

"Education of the Will," Jules Payot.

"Human Efficiency," Horatio W. Dresser.

"Getting the Most Out of Business," E. St. Elmo Lewis.

"Women of To-morrow," Wm. J. Hard.

"Woman and Labor," Olive Schreiner.

"Organization and Management Course," The Business Bourse, New York. (A course in self-education for executive work.)

"Emerson Course in Personal Efficiency," Emerson Institute, New York.

"Mental Efficiency," Arnold Bennett.

"Habit," William James.

"How to live on Twenty-four Hours a Day," Arnold Bennett.

"Memory and the Learning Process," D. O. Lyon.

"How to Get Your Pay Raised," Nathaniel Fowler.

"The Young Man in Business," Edward Bok.

"Fatigue and Inefficiency," Josephine Goldmark.

"Business Psychology," T. Sharper Knowlson.

"Psychology in Daily Life," Carl E. Seashore.

"Brain and Personality," Wm. Hanna Thomson.

"Binet-Simon Measuring Scale for Intelligence," S. C. Kohs.

"Psychological Methods of Testing Intelligence," W. Stern.

ON HEALTH AND PERSONAL INTERESTS

"Nutrition and Diet," Emma Conley.
"Keeping Physically Fit," Wm. J. Cromie.
"Exercises for Women," Florence Botton.
"Personal Hygiene and Physical Training for Women," Dr. Anna J. Galbraith.
"Cost of Living," Ellen H. Richards.
"Hygiene for the Worker," Tolman and Guthrie.
"Shelter and Clothing," Kinne and Cooley.
"Foods and Household Management," Kinne and Cooley.
"The New Housekeeping," Christine Frederick.
"Interior Decoration," Frank Alvah Parsons.
"Woman's Work in Municipalities," Mary Ritter Beard.
"American Woman in Civic Work," Helen C. Bennett.
"American Labor Unions," Helen Marot.
"Psychology of Relaxation," F. T. W. Patrick.
"How to Live," Irving Fisher.
"The Book of Thrift," T. D. MacGregor.
"Starving America," Alfred W. McCann.
"Health and Happiness," Dr. Eliza M. Mosher.
"Mind and Work," Luther H. Gulick.

OFFICE, CLERICAL AND ACCOUNTING; CREDIT AND COLLECTION

"Public Schools and Women in Office Service," Women's Industrial and Educational Union.
"The American Office," Wm. J. Schulze.
"Commercial Work and Training for Girls," Eaton and Stevens.
"A Reference Manual for Stenographers, Secretaries and Reporters," E. Banks.
"The Efficient Secretary," Ellen L. Spencer.
"Secretarial Work and Practice," Nixon and Richardson.
"Office Training for Stenographers," Rupert P. SoRelle.
"Indexing and Filing," E. R. Hudders.
"System" (Monthly), Chicago, Ill.
"Art of Collecting," A. J. Cassell.
"Mercantile Credits," Core, Elliott, Flatow.

"Gregg Writer" (Monthly), Chicago, Ill.
"Business" (Monthly), Detroit, Mich.
"Office Management," A. W. Shaw Co., Chicago.
"Accounts, Their Construction and Interpretation," Wm. Morse Cole.
"Dicksee's Auditing," R. H. Montgomery.
"Factory Costs," Webner.
"Theory and Practice of Higher Accounting," Henry Heitman.
"Accounting and Business Practice," J. H. Moore and Geo. Miner.
"Net Worth and the Balance Sheet," Herbert F. Stockwell.
"Accounting Every Business Man Should Know," E. E. Garrison.
"Business Education and Accountancy," C. W. Haskins.
"Your Slow Accounts—How to Collect Them," Beach.
"Distribution of Expense Burden," A. Hamilton Church.
"The Card System at the Office," J. Kaiser.
"How to Systematize a Day's Work," A. W. Shaw Co.

ECONOMICS AND FINANCE; STATISTICS

"What Every Business Woman Should Know," L. C. Kearney.
"Every-day Business for Women," Mary Aronetta Wilbur.
"A Handbook of Stock Exchange Laws," Samuel F. Goldman.
"Purchasing," C. S. Rindsfoos.
"Purchasing," H. B. Twyford.
"Commercial Paper," Roger W. Babson.
"Chemistry of Commerce," Robert M. Duncan.
"Theory of Business Enterprise," Veblen.
"Money, Exchange and Banking," Easton.
"International Commercial Policies," Fisk.
"Educational and Industrial Evolution," Carlton.
"Investment Bonds," Lownhaupt.
"Problems of To-day," Andrew Carnegie.
"Corporate Finance and Accounting," H. C. Bentley.

THE AMBITIOUS WOMAN IN BUSINESS

"Evolution of Industry," MacGregor.
"Trusts, Pools and Corporations," W. Z. Ripley.
"Elements of Transportation," E. R. Johnson.
"Railroad Administration," N. Morris.
"Economics of Business," Norris A. Brisco.
"Elements of Statistics," Arthur L. Bowley.
"Introduction to Statistics," George Yule.
"Babson's Statistical Service," published at Wellesley Hills, Mass.
"Banking and Insurance."
"History of Modern Banks of Issue," Chas. A. Conant.
"American Banker" (Weekly), New York.
"Financial World" (Weekly), New York.
"Dun's International Review" (Monthly), New York.

EXPORT AND TARIFF

"American Exporter" (Monthly), New York.
"Export American Industries" (Monthly), New York.
"Exporters & Importers Journal" (Monthly), New York.
"Tariff History of the United States," Prof. E. W. Taussig (Howard).
"Selling Latin America," W. E. Aughinbaugh.
"Round the World as a Special Salesman," A. E. Wright.

ENGLISH AND CORRESPONDENCE

"Desk-Book of Errors in English," Frank H. Vizetelly.
"How to Write Clearly," E. A. Abbott.
"Handbook of Modern Business Correspondence," Forrest Crissey.
"Effective Business Letters," Edwin H. Gardner.
"The Business Letter," Ion E. Dwyer.
"How to Write a Business Letter," Charles R. Wiers.
"The Art of Writing and Speaking the English Language," Sherwin Cody.
"Proofreading and Punctuation," Adele M. Smith.
"The Correct Word—How to Use It," Josephine T. Baker.
"How I Can Increase My Vocabulary," Josephine T. Baker.

"Business Correspondence and Manual of Dictation," William H. Brown.
"Writer's Desk Book," W. D. Orcutt.

ADVERTISING AND MAIL ORDER; TRADE JOURNALISM

"How to Deal with Human Nature in Business," Sherwin Cody.
"Advertisers' Handbook," International Correspondence Schools.
"Modern Advertising," Calkins & Holden.
"Science of Advertising," Edwin and Thomas Balmer.
"Forty Years an Advertising Agent," Geo. F. Rowell.
"Advertising as a Business Force," Prof. Paul T. Cherington (Harvard).
"Advertising Book of 1916," Prof. Paul T. Cherington (Harvard).
"Practical Publicity," Truman A. DeWeese.
"Psychology of Advertising," Walter Dill Scott.
"Theory of Advertising," Walter Dill Scott.
"Financial Advertising," E. St. Elmo Lewis.
"Art and Science of Advertising," George French.
"Analytical Advertising," F. A. Shryor.
"Ads and Sales," Herbert Casson.
"Principles of Appeal and Response," H. L. Hollingworth (Columbia).
"The New Business," Harry Tipper.
"Advertising—Its Principles and Practice," Hollingworth-Parsons-Tipper-Hotchkiss.
"Poster Advertising," G. H. E. Hawkins.
"Newspaper Advertising," G. H. E. Hawkins.
"Advertising—Selling the Consumer," John Lee Mahin.
"Writing an Advertisement," S. Roland Hall.
"How to Make Type Talk," B. D. Lewis.
"Productive Advertising, Herbert W. Hess (Univ. of Pa.).
"Letters that Make Good," Poole & Buzzell.
"Letters that Land Orders," John H. Lytle.

"Building Your Business by Mail," Wm. G. Clifford.

"The New Salesmanship and How to do Business by Mail," Chas. Lindgren.

"Planning an Advertising Campaign for a Manufacturer," (Univ. of Minnesota).

"How to Write a Business Letter," Charles R. Wiers.

"Principles of the Mail Order Business," Arthur E. Sweet.

"Industrial Journalism," Albert Frederick Wilson.

"Advertising and Selling" (monthly trade paper), New York.

"Printers' Ink" (weekly), New York.

"Associated Advertising" (monthly publication of the Associated Advertising Clubs of the World, Indianapolis, Ind.).

"Agricultural Advertising" (Monthly).

"Successful Selling by Mail," Randolph Rose School, Chattanooga, Tenn.

"Selling Newspaper Space," Joseph E. Chasnoff.

"Scientific Circulation Management for Newspapers," William R. Scott.

"Advertising and Progress," Hole and Hart, London.

"Report of Merchandising Investigation conducted by Associated Advertising Clubs," Mac Martin, Minneapolis.

"News, Ads and Sales," B. J. Opdycke.

"The Principles of Advertising Arrangement," Frank Alvah Parsons.

"An Advertising Manual for People Who Write Their Own Ads," J. R. Wheeler.

"Bank Advertising Plans," T. D. MacGregor.

"Bank Advertising," M. M. Rothschild.

"How to Get the Want Ads," H. Doorly.

"How a Retail Merchant Should Advertise," Merchants Adv. & Supply Co., Statesville, N. C.

"The Premium System of Forcing Sales," H. S. Bunting.

"Specialty Advertising—the new way to Build Business," H. S. Bunting.

"Town Promotion and Municipal Advertising," Morton Eichman Co.

"Principles of Successful Church Advertising," C. Stelzle.
"The House Organ; How to Make it Produce Results."
"How to Advertise Printing," H. M. Basford.
"Church Publicity," C. F. Reisner.
"Moving Picture Theatre Advertising," E. W. Sargent.
"Successful Restaurant Publicity," M. E. Westbrooke.

PRINTING

"Preparation of Manuscripts for the Printer," Frank H. Vizetelly.
"Color and Its Application to Printing," Miller.
"Manual of Style" (pub. by University of Chicago).
"Dictionary of Engraving," Baker.
"Chart—Relative Adaptability of Printing Plates," Baker.
"Typography of Advertising," F. J. Tresize.
"Art and Practice of Typography," E. C. Gross.
"Decorative Designs," Paul N. Hasbeck.
"How to Compile a Catalog," C. G. Wasson.
"Some Notes on Catalog Making," S. Graydon.

SELLING AND TEXTILES

"Economies of Retailing," Paul H. Nystrom.
"Salesmanship for Women," Adelaide Benedict-Roche.
"Saleswomen in Mercantile Stores," E. B. Butler.
"Successful Selling," E. Leichter.
"How to Run a Store at a Profit," System Pub. Co., Chicago.
"Manual of Successful Storekeeping," W. R. Hotchkin.
"Human Nature in Selling Goods," Jas. H. Collins.
"Men Who Sell Things," Walter L. Moody.
"Fifty Years on the Road, E. P. Briggs.
"A. B. C. of Salesmanship," F. P. Rush.
"Influencing Men in Business," Prof. Walter Dill Scott.
"Salesmanship, Deportment and System," W. A. Corbion.
"Talks by the Old Storekeeper," Frank Farrington.
"Making of a Merchant," Harlow E. Higginbottom.
"Retail Advertising Complete," Frank Farrington.

"Retail Selling and Store Management," Paul H. Nystrom.
"Textiles," Paul H. Nystrom.
"What a Salesman Should Know," H. C. Taylor.
"Short Talks on Retail Selling," S. Roland Hall.
"Reducing Cost of Selling for Dept. Stores," A. G. Chaney.
"Breezy—a clerk's story," J. George Frederick.
"Success in Retailing," Butler Bros., Chicago.
"A Dictionary of Men's Wear," W. H. Baker.
"Sales Plans," T. A. Bird.
"Store Management," Frank Farrington.
"The Clerk's Book," Frank Farrington.
"Selling Suggestions," Frank Farrington.
"Making a Drug Store Pay," Frank Farrington.
"How to Conduct a Successful Shoe Store," C. L. Garrison.
"The Art of Retail Selling—a Text-book for Salespeople," D. Hirschler.
"Salesmanship," W. M. Maxwell.
"Automobile Business," J. H. Newmark.
"Economics of Retailing," Paul H. Nystrom.
"The Merchandising of Textiles," C. C. Parlin.
"How Department Stores are Carried On," W. B. Phillips.
"Keeping up with Rising Costs," W. Sammons.
"How to Sell Hardware," R. F. Soule.
"How to Become a Successful Salesman," G. W. Stearns.
"The Complete Storekeeper," N. I. White.
"The Psychology of a Sale," H. A. Forbes-Lindsay.
"Psychology of Soliciting," J. I. Harden.
"Dry Goods Economist" (Weekly), New York.
"Lace & Embroidery Review" (Monthly), New York.
"Textile Colorist" (Monthly), Philadelphia.
"American Wool & Cotton Reporter" (Weekly), Boston.
"Textile World Record" (Monthly), Boston.
"Woman's Wear" (Daily and Weekly), New York.
"American Carpet & Upholstery Journal" (Monthly), Philadelphia.
"Housefurnishing Review" (Monthly), New York.

"Illustrated Milliner" (Monthly), New York.
"Milliner" (Monthly), Chicago.
"Merchants' Record & Show Window" (Monthly), Chicago.
"Novelty News" (Monthly), Chicago.

SCIENTIFIC MANAGEMENT AND BUSINESS PRINCIPLES

"Twelve Principles of Efficiency," Harrington Emerson.
"Efficiency as a Basis for Operation and Wages," Harrington Emerson.
"Principles of Scientific Management," Frederick W. Taylor.
"Profit-making in Shop or Factory Management," C. V. Carpenter.
"Factory Organization and Administration," Hugo Diemer.
"Human Factor in Works Management," J. Hartness.
"Fatigue Study," Frank and Lillian Gilbreth.
"Psychology and Industrial Efficiency," Hugo Muensterberg.
"Motion Study," Frank Gilbreth.
"Primer of Scientific Management," Frank Gilbreth.
"Work, Wages and Profit," H. L. Gantt.
"Bonus Systems of Rewarding Labor," H. L. Gantt.
"Production Factors," A. Hamilton Church.
"Applied Methods of Scientific Management," Frederick A. Parkhurst.
"Factory Management," Frank A. Arnold.
"Works Management," W. Duane Ennis.
"Shop Management," Frederick W. Taylor.
"Scientific Management," Papers read at the Tuck School Conference, Dartmouth.
"Scientific Management and the Railroads," Louis D. Brandeis.
"Cost-keeping and Scientific Management," H. A. Evans.

LEGAL WELFARE AND REFERENCE WORKS

"Laws of Unfair Competition," Harry D. Nims.
"Laws of Advertising and Sales," Clowry Chapman.
"American Business Law with Legal Forms," J. J. Sullivan.
"Property Insurance," R. S. Huebner.
"Good-will, Trade-marks and Unfair Trading," Edward S. Rogers.
"Price Maintenance," Thomas A. Fernley.
"Concentration and Control" (on Price Maintenance), Chas. R. Van Hise.
"Patents," Prindle.
"Industrial Accident Prevention," D. S. Beyer.
"Health of the Worker," Metrop. Life Ins. Co.
"The Modern Factory," G. M. Price.
"Employers Welfare Work," U. S. Bureau of Labor Statistics.
"Safety-Methods of Preventing Occupational Accidents," Tolman & Kendall.
"Business Barometers," Roger W. Babson.
"Mahin's Data Book," Mahin Advertising Agency, Chicago.
(This contains names of trade papers for every industry, as well as other data.)
"Law of Commercial Papers," Leslie J. Tompkins.
"Commercial Correspondence and Postal Information," C. L. Altmaier

LIBERAL ARTS COLLEGES THAT INCLUDE BUSINESS COURSES (Open to Women)

New York University School of Commerce and Finance, New York.
Columbia University, New York.
Rockford College, Rockford, Ill.
Connecticut College for Women, New London, Conn.
James Milliken University, Decatur, Ill.
Indiana University, Bloomington, Ind.
Boston University, Boston, Mass.
Simmons College, Boston, Mass.

INDEX

INDEX

INDEX